MW01094620

1

INTRODUCTION

This is the story of Mary Duncan Crandall, who was born soon after the American Civil War in the eastern United States to a poor, circuit-riding preacher man and his diminutive wife on the frontiers of eastern North Carolina. With little chance for an education and multitudes of chores to perform on their little cotton farm, what were the prospects for a little red-haired girl in the days of the carpetbaggers and reconstruction in the South? It would be a life of utter poverty, the family perpetually financially destitute. She was the last of the 12 babies to be born to this loving couple, only eight of whom would survive to adulthood. How could she expect to become anybody who would leave even the faintest impression on her generation, let alone the generations to follow? Well, her story is one of hope, shattered lives and dreams, poverty and visions to be fulfilled. But let's not get ahead of our story. Let's start with the little we know about Mary's grandparents...

Alfred Duncan married Mary Edith Carroll on July 8th 1832 in Sampson County, North Carolina when that region of the country was still frontier. To place the time frames in context it must be understood that these were pioneering people who were born soon after the War of 1812. America was a very young nation. This was still fewer than 50 years after the United States Constitution was signed. This great experiment in representative democracy that was the United States of America had just been launched.

Alfred was a farmer in North Carolina. His father, Dugald Duncan, came from a Scottish family. He married Edith Ann Chesnutt. Henry Duncan was Edith and Alfred's son who was born on October 10, 1846. That would make him 17 years old when he entered the Civil War in 1863.

Nathan and Julia Boon Bell also moved their family to the eastern part of North Carolina. Their daughter, Eliza Jane Bell, was born September 22, 1848. Eliza Bell and Harry Duncan were destined to meet some time after Harry returned from the Civil War.

Here is their story....

Civil War

It seemed that all the violence, hate and destruction of hell itself had broken loose. The last defenses of the old South were crumbling. Atlanta fell to Sherman's Army in early September 1864. He devoted the next few weeks to chasing Confederate troops through northern Georgia in a vain attempt to lure them into a decisive fight. The Confederate's evasive tactics doomed Sherman's plan to achieve victory on the battlefield so he developed an alternative strategy: destroy the South by laying waste to its economic and transportation infrastructure.

Sherman's "scorched earth" campaign began on November 15th when he cut the last telegraph wire that linked him to his superiors in the North. He left Atlanta in flames and pointed his army south. No word would be heard from him for the next five weeks. Unbeknownst to his enemy, Sherman's objective was the port of Savannah. His army of 65,000 cut a broad swath as it lumbered toward its destination. Plantations were burned, crops destroyed and stores of food pillaged. In the wake of his progress to the sea he left numerous "Sherman sentinels" (the chimneys of burnt out houses) and "Sherman neckties" (railroad rails that had been heated and wrapped around trees.)

Along the way, his army was joined by thousands of former slaves who brought up the rear of the march because they had no other place to go. Sherman's army reached Savannah on December 22, 1864. Two days later, Sherman telegraphed President Lincoln with the message "I beg to present to you, as a Christmas gift, the city of Savannah..."

General Sherman's army had not been stopped and was sweeping through as Henry Joshua Duncan waited expectantly with his fellow confederate recruits in North Carolina. The reverberations of this marching army were felt deep in the soul of every single Southerner ... pandemonium reigned ... boys, old men, almost everyone was being

4

recruited for a last ditch stand near Fayetteville. That last-ditch stand never happened. Sherman's army bypassed Fayetteville and the surrounding area altogether on his march to the sea. He wanted nothing to slow him down.

It was the beginning of the end for the Confederacy. Sherman had stayed in Savannah until the end of January and then continued his scorched earth campaign through the Carolinas. On April 26, 1865, Confederate troops under General Joseph E. Johnston surrendered to Sherman in North Carolina; seventeen days after Lee surrendered to Grant at Appomattox.

Henry J. Duncan was only 14 years old when the Civil War broke out. He followed the war with great attention, and three years later on July 16, 1863, at just seventeen years old, he enlisted in Company B, 2nd Infantry Battalion, to defend the honor of the Confederacy. It was toward the end of the war, but the Confederate army was so desperate that they took every able body available. Henry was really too young for battle. With no training, but with a musket thrust into his hands, he had been shoved into the trenches as a replacement. While Henry and the Confederate army waited for General Sherman, who never came, a most remarkable Baptist evangelist, with a fury and fire equal to the dreaded General, did come. He preached like a man from another world to those ragged, hungry, tired soldiers down in the dirty trenches. Henry Duncan became one of his converts.

The dreadful war ended - the battlefields were cleared of dead and wounded - the soldiers disbanded and went home to... nothing. However, it was different with Henry Duncan. While he, like the others, was going home to nothing, he was also taking something wonderful along with him. Since Henry had a personal encounter with Jesus Christ, he had a deep conviction that he, too, must now preach the Gospel. So Henry Joshua Duncan (born October 10, 1846) was not just another poor cotton farmer during the reconstruction days of the South. Indeed, he was a poor cotton farmer, but he became first a Baptist Minister and second, a poor cotton farmer.

Henry felt called to preach, so he came back home and began to prepare for the ministry. His father gave him a piece of wooded land and he cleared enough to make room to build a small log cabin house. Henry built the cabin himself; constructed of the trees he cleared from the little parcel of wooded land his father had given him.

Eventually Henry met Eliza Jane Bell (born September 22, 1848), who would become the love of his life. She was a sprite of a little thing. But she was of stern pioneer stock, small but strong and full of life with excitement and optimism for the future. The night of their wedding Henry carried his beautiful bride over the threshold of his new cabin. That first night of their marriage, they both knelt on the rough cabin floor, and by the soft glow of candlelight, dedicated their lives to God. They asked his blessing on their home and the children that they hoped would come later.

The prayer that began that evening was to continue daily, without interruption, for the next half a century. They asked God to bless them and help them. And, He certainly did. Theirs was just the beginning of a story that would impact much of the eastern part of the fledgling United States for the Kingdom of God.

Henry Duncan went on to become a great preacher and Justice of the Peace. He and Eliza worked hard on the farm as they were raising cotton and a vegetable garden and all else to meet the needs of a rapidly growing family. Out of necessity, all the children who eventually were born into this marriage had to work on the farm. They canned the food in the summer and they ate it in the winter. They made the biscuits from scratch and there was very little buying of groceries in those days. They lived very close to the land. Living in this little cabin in the woods of North Carolina, Henry and Elizabeth never had breakfast by the light of day. They were always up before daybreak with the candlelight for breakfast in order to be ready in time for chores in the farm. That's how they survived, with tremendous hard work in the fields and in the farmyard.

Henry and Eliza Duncan

Henry J. Duncan

These were the children of this Godly union between Henry and Eliza:

- Lou Sulia (1867 - 1943)

- William Henry (1869 - 1930)

- Annie Eliza (1870 - 1905)

- Addie Bell (1872 - 1940)

- Nathan Guy (1874 - 1939)

- Alfred (1876 - 1876)

- John Murphy (1878 -1966)

- Julia Jane (1880 -1952)

- Florence Edith (1882 - 1963)

- Jimmie (1884 - 1885)

- Bettie Laura (1886 - 1905)

- Mary Jane (1888 - 1971)

Eliza Jane Duncan

(Eliza's mother, Julia Boon Bell, who also never weighed more than one hundred pounds in her life, had given birth to ten children of her own. Two died when they were very young. Julia also later raised five of her grandchildren whose mother had died. Julia lived until May 1913 and passed away in her mid-80s when Mary was 25 years old.) These were strong, frontier, pioneering people!

In the early years Eliza made all the cloth the family needed, both wool and cotton, as well as all the family's clothes, including Henry's preaching suit. The family planted and grew their own cotton. There were no clothing stores to shop in, nor any money to make purchases, even if there had been a store nearby. The family lived off the land, and there was always work to be done. All of the children were involved with chores and helping with the care of the farm animals on a daily basis. No time for leisure, and barely any for a formal education.

Every Friday at noon, Henry would take off his dirty old farm clothes and have a hot bath, hitch up his best mule and buggy and put on this preaching suit. He would say goodbye to his wife and the children and disappear down the old dirt road in a great cloud of dust, headed for his preaching stations. Henry would preach from Saturday mornings through Sunday mornings as he was traveling in a circuit to different locales as an itinerant preacher. He would drive his circuit every weekend and preach at these churches and come back on Sunday evening on his horse and buggy. As the years passed by Henry would become known as one of the key leaders of the Baptist church movement in eastern North Carolina. Several churches were planted as a direct and indirect result of his pioneering leadership in eastern North Carolina.

Mary is born

This was the home in which Mary Duncan was to be born... God was honored and served ... hard work was the order of the day. Mary Duncan began her life in 1888, on a hot, dusty, sultry afternoon, the 19th of August, on the old cotton farm near Roseboro, North Carolina. Eliza Duncan had given birth to her twelfth, and last, child. Henry and Eliza decided their new round-faced, red-haired daughter would be named Mary Jane. She was to be the last child born to Henry and Eliza, and was youngest of the nine surviving children. She lived on the farm and as she grew up she only went to school a few months out of the year because she was born in 1888 when the frontier of the south was in a very poor condition, and she was needed at home to help with all the chores.

Harry Duncan with all his family at the time (about 1873), wife Eliza, Mother-in-Law Julia Bell and children Lou, William, Annie and Addie

It was also not a priority for women at that time to attend school in this pioneering culture in the South. Although her education was very limited, she was an excellent student and remembered her grammar skills long into her later life. (Her grandchildren well remember when Mary heard one of her grandchildren using the wrong tense of a verb that she was sure to correct that child.)

But her older sister Florence was the beneficiary of a good formal education. Florence was legally blind, so she was sent to the school for the blind. A blind girl doesn't make a very good farm hand, so she was able to leave home for long enough periods of time to complete her schooling. She performed so well at school that she was asked to come back and be a teacher for the blind, which she did for a few years. Mary's brothers were fortunate to receive a good deal more education than was afforded Mary. John went to Bible School and became a pastor, and one of the nephews, Stacy, became a doctor.

So Mary grew up in this loving and happy rural family where each member had his own responsibilities and the family worked together in love, peace and harmony. However, this calm orderly rural farm life was not to continue past her youth for Mary Duncan - when she was still a teenager she was to have a dramatic experience that would change her entire life, and as a result, the lives of thousands of others, forever. She was about to suffer the worst kind of rejection and discrimination, a kind that would have devastated a weaker person, but would somehow prove to be the springboard to launch an exciting future for this young lady. Strength is often born of adversity, and that would be the case in Mary's life.

The Turning Point

But we have to backtrack a little... When dawn came on January 1, 1900, Mary was a young girl of twelve years. Also, this new day brought the world into the twentieth century! With it came a new optimism for this young nation. The future looked bright... slavery had been outlawed, the frontier was being tamed and the country looked westward for its future. Industry was developing in the south and new jobs were being created every day. There was no reason to suspect that within the churches of America events would soon take place that would forever change the future of many of the citizens of this country.

The spiritual climate of the young nation was mixed during those years. The Protestant churches dominated the country and there was only a very small Roman Catholic presence. And non-Christian churches were almost unheard of. There was a genuine evangelistic fervor among the Baptist churches in the Carolinas in those days. In fact, Pastor Henry Duncan would plant several Baptist churches in North Carolina and eventually was overseer of a group of churches in this territory. But the broader mainline Protestant churches in America in the nineteenth century were becoming wealthy, cultured and influential. Their spiritual state was low and their worship was tepid. The twentieth century protestant church seemed not to be very focused on taking the gospel to the world. The elaborately dressed choirs would deliver very artistic performances but the spirituality seemed cold and not focused on a vision to take salvation to a lost world.

It was extraordinary, that, at this same time, great revivals led by evangelists like Charles Finney and Dwight Moody would create a spiritual paradox in this country. The increased fervor brought about by their revival movements seemed to create a great momentum to take the gospel to the whole world. But this new spiritual wave did not find a willing home in the traditional mainline Protestant churches of that period. The concept of being 'separated from the world' was not attractive to these traditional churches that had found social acceptability more comfortable than evangelism.

In the midst of this mixed climate there began a strong 'Holiness' movement in the northeastern United States in the late 1800s. As a result of its focus, teaching separate living and strict standards of conduct and creating a divergence from traditional denominations, the Holiness revivals led frequently to the organization of independent churches. These Holiness groups spread from the northeast into the south and Midwest giving rise to new, independent churches by the dawn of the twentieth century. This new spiritual force brought a fresh breath of revival that was beginning to dawn upon America.

Mary Jane Duncan officially joined the Baptist Church in White Oak, North Carolina sometime after 1893. She was baptized in water in the White Oak area by her father, Reverend Henry J. Duncan. However, it should be noted that Mary said that she never had a 'know-so' salvation until 1907 when she had the experiences related below during the Pentecostal movement.

Out of the holiness movement the modern Pentecostal movement had its birth in 1900 in Topeka, Kansas. Rev. Charles Parham had opened Bethel Bible College. One day in autumn of 1900, he asked his students to study diligently for the next several weeks everything the Bible said about the evidence of receiving the baptism in the Holy Spirit. On the first day of 1901 the Holy Spirit came upon the first student; this young lady immediately began to speak in tongues to glorify God, and this

14

experience soon spread to others in the class. The Day of Pentecost had come again onto this small campus, one of the first cases known in modern times. And this rose to become a groundswell of momentum as new revival began to dawn on this country.

Subsequently, Charles Parham and others began to conduct revival meetings in cities across America. It was in Charles Parham's meetings in Houston, Texas, where more than 25,000 were saved. In those meetings in 1905 a black Holiness preacher named William J. Seymour would experience this same baptism in the Holy Spirit. And his travels would soon take him to Los Angeles, California.

Revival – a Fire Breaks Out

It was there, in a little two story framed structure on Azuza Street in an industrial district of Los Angeles that William J. Seymour was conducting a service for Baptists who were seeking a deeper experience with God. On April 9, 1906, during one of these meetings the entire company was knocked out of their seats onto the floor as if hit by a bolt of lightning. Immediately, seven among them began to speak in other tongues. Their shouting was so loud and fervent that a crowd gathered outside wondering "what meaneth this", just as the crowd had done on the Day of Pentecost almost two thousand years before in Acts 2:4. There would be a constant revival in that place for the next three years. Many came from across America and foreign countries to see and experience this powerful move of God.

This revival that began in the small frame building in Los Angeles, California was destined to shake the entire religious world. Although the revival had its roots all the way back to Scotland and within the USA to Topeka, Kansas, it seems to have ignited in Azuza Street with a fire so bright that its glow would spread across the whole of the United States and could not be extinguished. Soon it became apparent that this great revival would sweep across the whole country at the beginning of the twentieth century. By January of 1907, this Great Pentecostal Revival that began in California had spread to North Carolina. Soon this revival and Mary

Duncan would cross paths, and it would change forever the direction of young Mary Duncan's life. Specifically, these meetings in Azuza Street in Los Angeles would make a significant imprint on Mary Duncan Crandall's entire life story.

Many within the church heard the news about this mighty outpouring of the Holy Spirit revival that started on Azuza Street in Los Angeles, CA in 1906. A North Carolina evangelist by the name of Rev. G. B. Cashwell heard about the revival and went out to Los Angeles to see for himself what it was all about. He heard much about this great sovereign outpouring of the Holy Spirit of God going on there. So, once he heard about it, he took the train and went to Los Angeles immediately. He was so moved by what he heard that he just wired his wife in North Carolina and headed west to experience the great revival in Los Angeles for himself. He was there for a number of days and experienced the infilling of the Holy Spirit himself, and when he returned, he brought the Holy Spirit fire with him. He immediately began to hold meetings in his home state of North Carolina. When he came back home to North Carolina, the second meeting he conducted was at Zoar Church near Roseboro, North Carolina (now Zoar Pentecostal Free Will Baptist Church in Salemburg, North Carolina)

According to Benjamin Crandall, "Mama's oldest sister Aunt Lou Cooper lived in Roseboro, and mother went to visit her during this revival meeting when she was about eighteen years old. Betty Louise (Aunt Lou) had attended the first meeting and came home excited and began to tell her sister all about it. The following evening both Mary and Aunt Lou attended the Cashwell meeting together".

Mary had never seen anything like those meetings in her life. The joy of the Lord in these people simply overwhelmed her. She thought they called it 'Pentecost' but the name actually meant nothing to her. It was an experience with God that she wanted more than anything in this world. During this meeting there was such joy and wonderful presence of God that Mary proclaimed, "These people have something that I don't have and that I want..." It was truly something she profoundly desired and began to ask God for in a new way.

As Mary continued to wait quietly in prayer before the Lord after returning to her sister Lou's home, searching questions penetrated her mind and soul, demanding an answer. It was as if Jesus were speaking to her personally: "Are you willing to be put out of your home for Me? Are you willing to be misunderstood for My sake, to be despised and persecuted for My sake? Are you willing for folks to put you out, and to be ostracized, and to be rejected because of this experience and because of receiving Me and my blessing?"   The answers didn't come quickly. Then the penetrating voice returned, quoting Matthew 10:32: "If you love father or mother more than Me, you are not worthy of Me. If you are ashamed of Me, I will be ashamed of you. Blessed are ye when men shall revile you and persecute you and say all manner of evil against you falsely for My sake. Rejoice and be exceeding glad for great is your reward in heaven. For so persecuted they the prophets who were before you."

So, in response, Mary finally said, "Yes, whatever it takes, I'm willing!" Immediately the power of the Lord fell upon Mary. She began to dance and to shout and to speak in tongues! She had never heard of this before and did not know what to call it... but she knew she had received some great power and anointing she never had experienced before.

"Well," Mary thought, "Lord, if getting more of You causes people to put me out of their homes, and causes me to be rejected; if I must choose between man and God, You are my choice. For I want you more than life itself." The contract was made. It was never to be broken. That young and lovely girl of eighteen, kneeling on the floor of her sister Lou's home that night, little realized how true and prophetic those words were going to be. Mary had made the consecration and that same Sunday afternoon at her sister's home the answer came. That same joy Mary had seen in other people came to her. Praise and worship to God sprang spontaneously from her innermost being! She began to praise God in languages other than English without even realizing what she was doing

... languages she had never learned. Later, Mary eventually realized she had received what the Bible called the "Baptism of the Holy Spirit."

Within a few days she returned home and almost immediately became a controversial figure. This would continue to be the case with her for the rest of her life. In the years ahead she would be loved and hated, praised and cursed, understood and misunderstood, approved and criticized, honored and walked on and even physically abused for her standing up for her Savior. Few persons who knew her were ever neutral ... her life was destined to pass through great storms. Truly her faith would be tested: would those chains of love, forged that night by the white heat of God's love, hold true?

Growing up Very Fast

The news of what was happening at Zoar Church spread like a wildfire through the communities surrounding Salemburg, North Carolina. Mary's father, Henry Duncan, was slow to pass judgment, but in time the influential religious leaders, many of whom were his Baptist friends and colleagues, wore him down. He became persuaded his daughter had been dreadfully deceived and was into fanaticism. The religious leaders were quietly applying pressure and awaiting the outcome. Her brother, who was finishing his studies, was summoned home. Surely, he would help talk Mary out of this thing, so they thought. In those days you couldn't be disrespectful in answering back, you just had to listen in respect to your parents. They spoke to her and told her how these people were fanatics, that this wasn't God.

When finally Mary was allowed to speak, she said, "You all have come too late. I already have this experience and this has already happened to me." A few days later, when every effort failed, he gave Mary his ultimatum. With obvious pain in his voice, her father said to her, "Mary, you have a choice. You can either stop going to those meetings, or leave home. I have made up my mind - you will not be allowed to remain at home and attend those Pentecostal meetings. Think it over and let me know your decision..."

18

The decision wasn't easy. She loved her parents dearly and besides, where could she go? She was only 18. Then she remembered the words the night of her consecration "Are you willing to have your mother and father forsake you and to be put out of your home for My sake?" She remembered her answer that night - "Lord, You are my choice." At the appropriate time she gave them her decision, packed her few belongings, she said goodbye and walked out. But not alone! Jesus was beside her. So, Mary packed her bags at age eighteen and stepped out! She would have to stay with other friends for a while. So, what was to become of Mary Duncan, with no home, no income, no skills to earn a living and now estranged from her family?

(A footnote is appropriate here: Mary's father, Pastor Henry Duncan, was a good man who loved God. After observing Mary's commitment to the Lord and the power and faith in which she moved, a year or two later Pastor Henry stood up in the Baptist church and publicly said, "I have a confession to make because I was wrong. My daughter has something that I don't have in her relationship with the Lord. I was wrong, and I have to acknowledge this." So, he invited Mary to come back home and said, "I was wrong! What you have IS from God!") However, she never did come back home to live because... well, you have to read on to see what happens next.

Mary Crandall's Vision

Sometimes God uses strange circumstances to bring His will to pass, and this was one of those times. The day Mary stepped out and said, "Goodbye," she was saying goodbye to more than her parents - she was saying goodbye forever to her childhood ... the parental care, the sheltered life on the cotton farm. That comfortable family life would never return and that was the day Mary grew up! Ahead, there was a courageous and adventurous life to be lived, with battles to be fought and wars to be won, great rivers to be forded and high mountains to be scaled. She, like Pilgrim from the book, "Pilgrim's Progress," had set her face toward heaven like a flint and there was to be no turning back. Mary prayed much in those days, and many times fasted days at a time. It was during this period that she had a remarkable experience that, in many ways, was similar to

General Booth's, the founder of the Salvation Army. It would imprint her life forever!

General Booth had a vision of eternity that drastically altered the course of his life and transformed General Booth into one of the greatest soul-winners of all time. The Salvation Army was established from that experience. Likewise, Mother's experience transformed her from a shy, bashful, sheltered child to a courageous, daring, relentless soul-winner.

The vision she had that day in 1908 was a transformative experience that would never leave her. It seemed to be a type of death although she wasn't sick and actually did not die. As she was praying, she experienced her breath getting shorter and shorter, and the sensation of her soul leaving her body and going into the outer darkness of eternity, forever lost and without hope. The experience lasted a long time, it seemed. During this vision she saw the end of the world ... the moon turned to blood and the stars fell from heaven. And she looked into the depths of hell itself!

Then the Holy Spirit spoke to her and said, "Go, warn them to flee from the wrath to come. Go! Go!" Later, she realized she had experienced a vision of hell and of the very end of the world. The effect of this vision on her was so totally consuming that she started going out immediately from house to house, knocking on people's doors, asking them to give her the opportunity to speak to them about their souls. Many were gloriously converted. Others were deeply convicted. Still others were outraged by her interruptions and rejected her just as people had done to Jesus in Bible days.

Up until this time Mary had never seen or heard of a woman minister, and preaching was the farthest thought from her mind. But, invitations began to come to her from everywhere. She had no model to look to for developing her approach to ministry. There were no women pastors or preachers... and few women evangelists. Mary was totally dependent on hearing clear direction from the Holy Spirit to plan and direct all of her ministry activities. She would just pray, and pray, and pray until she heard from the Lord what she was to do. Then she would ask Him for the resources to do it, and then off she went, obeying His instructions. She did not know better. And there was no better way to conduct her life and ministry. It was often said that Mary always heard from the Lord and there were not many surprises. She always seemed to know what was coming next.

Baptist churches opened their doors to her. Methodist groups got together and sponsored her meetings. Schoolhouses were opened to her. Wherever she went, revival seemed to follow. She was as surprised as everyone else, when she later realized that God, who is no respecter of persons, had given her the gift of evangelism. It all came so very simply to her. The doors opened, and though no one in that part of the country had ever seen - or heard of - a woman minister, Mary never let it stop her! She faced much opposition from the organized religious world in isolation, all by herself. She just didn't fit into their little box of religious traditions. Her youngest son, Ben Crandall, remarked that he had always thought that his mother, Mary Duncan, "...was way ahead of her time!"

Cora Garris and Mary Duncan

Mary began to travel and take this new message of hope wherever she found an open door. It was about that time that she met another woman who felt called to a life of evangelism and was herself a strong, praying woman. So Mary began taking Cora Garris with her, and they went all around the eastern part of North Carolina holding meetings. And it seemed that immediately the doors began to open for them because they been willing to obey and step out! They began to go place to place praying, speaking and evangelizing. Churches began to open up for them, even prominent churches such as the Methodist Churches. During Mary's ministry there and for the next several years a number of churches were started. Everyone she met, everywhere she went, she was passing out tracts (pamphlets about Jesus) and witnessing for the Lord. She was a natural born evangelist in telling others about Christ, and had such a passion for prayer! God's hand was upon her life in an unusual way, and soon doors of opportunity for her to minister opened throughout the entire state. It has been documented that, as a direct result of her ministry, at least seven churches were established in North Carolina alone.

It was amazing to see different churches opening up to invite them to come and hold meetings in their sanctuaries. They would hold meetings in old fashioned brush arbors, also in churches and in people's homes. (Brush arbors were common outside meetings in the south. They were held near trees and brush for covering during the day and sometimes nearby fires were burning for warmth in the evenings.)

This young Mary Crandall was a fiery redhead who was truly on fire for God along with her prayer partner and fellow traveling evangelist, Cora Garris! Many churches were started from some of those very early meetings. They prayed, they fasted, they sought God and tremendous things happened wherever they went. It was a lifestyle of prayer! They would pray all day and then minister all night. They had an amazing fervor for the things of God! All the people who ever really knew Mary would immediately think about the word, "prayer" any time they thought about her.

Mary knew her education left much to be desired, but she only hungered for more of God and His Holy Word. So, Mary attended the Holmes Bible and Missionary Institute in Greenville, South Carolina for a short period of time. It was during this period of her life that Mary felt a call of God to become a missionary to China. She believed her schooling at Holmes would prepare the way for this work. In fact, the Falcon Pentecostal Holiness Church collected a love offering for her to help support this cause. Mary has a close friend, Maggie Gaylor Kelley, who had become a missionary in China, but she and all of her children died there. Even so, Mary had saved up her fare and was about ready to go when events brought an abrupt end to her plans. The Boxer Rebellion had begun several years earlier in China and at this time China not only turned down all new American immigrants, but also sent all current American missionaries to China back home.

So she continued preaching for the Pentecostal Baptists along with other denominations throughout the North Carolina area. These two dedicated praying ladies, Mary and Cora, were very aware of being led by the Spirit of the Lord wherever they went! All their direction came from the Spirit. There was no structure anywhere or anyone to lead them or to show them the way. It was only by the Spirit of God. It was not unlike the book of Acts where Paul travelled from city to city, as the Holy Spirit told him where to go and when to stay.

It was not long before Mary was preaching in organized meetings, with crowds up to one-thousand persons, and sometimes to small groups in someone's home. But she never, ever stopped witnessing personally to people. To those closest to her this was the most outstanding part of her ministry. Few have ever met anyone quite like her. Mary's trademark was her handbag full of "tracts". Her whole purpose in life was to win people to Christ ... she literally spoke to everyone about the Lord, and usually gave them a tract.

She seemed to float about from place to place holding Holy Ghost meetings. Although it is well documented that she was responsible for at least six or seven churches being planted in eastern North Carolina, who knows how many others were planted in New England and New York? Mother Crandall became a member of the Dunn Assembly of God church in N.C., but she frequently attended the little Pentecostal Holiness church in Falcon, N.C. There is a stained glass window dedicated to Mary Crandall with her name on it at the Assembly of God church in Dunn, NC today!

Bible School in New England

It was sometime around the turn of the century when a young faith preacher by the name of Rev. E. W. Kenyon began holding some teaching and healing meetings in Framingham, Massachusetts. As these meetings grew in attendance, he began opening his home for teaching and boarding students. It wasn't long before this led to Kenyon opening a small Bible School in 1900 in the town of Spencer Mass, just about five miles away from Framingham, Mass. This was to be a faith believing type of Bible school, whereby the students would not have to carry the expenses of housing and classes, but they would all believe in faith for the money to come in from outside sources as they trusted in the Lord to provide for the income to run the school and pay for the expenses. It was later to become Bethel Bible Institute.

Mary was very excited in 1912 when she heard about this school and began earnestly praying about whether she should attend Bethel Bible Institute in Massachusetts. She had no money to get there, but somehow God miraculously provided the money for her to get there. So in 1913, at the age of 25, she packed up all her clothing items in a suitcase and moved north to attend Bethel Bible Institute in Spencer, Mass. This was to be the high point in Mary's formal education, because of her limited high school days back in North Carolina when she was helping on the farm. She roomed with another young lady named Frederica Peck at Bethel Bible Institute.

It was here in Spencer, Massachusetts where she attended Bethel Bible Institute for one whole year in 1913 and 1914, that Mary was exposed to the Word of Faith teachings that enabled her Bible training to merge with her experience in walking within the Holy Spirit's power and healing grace. Mary was now 26 years old. She came north with no money and graduated with her school paid in full. It was her first experience with a faith walk in which she learned that 'when God calls, He will provide'. Every time money was needed she somehow (miraculously) was provided with the money that was needed. It was a lesson that she would draw from the remainder of her life.

It was while attending Bethel Bible Institute that Mary heard about a healing evangelist by the name of Maria Woodsworth Etter. She was holding some meetings in the town of Framingham, Massachusetts, near Bethel Bible Institute. Maria Etter began a series of meetings in which she ministering to these people in downtown Framingham, anointing them with "oil," and praying for healing to take place in the name of Jesus. Healings and miracles truly began to take place! Before long Mary was very much enjoying attending and participating in these one on one evangelism and healing outreaches in towns nearby.

It was in the town of Montwait, Massachusetts, near the bible school, when policemen came and shut down the meetings and street ministry. The authorities were claiming these evangelists were practicing unauthorized medicine, because of using the anointing oil on the foreheads of those they prayed for. Maria Etter was put on trial for violating the law because she was not a doctor, and the police accused her of illegally practicing medicine. Mary Duncan, it was told, was one of the witnesses on her behalf. Many testified of God's healing of their bodies and finally the judge gave up and just threw the case completely out of court! Truly, he said, this is "pure religion and you cannot stop it".

A little later on, in the Maria Woodsworth Etter meetings in Zebulon, North Carolina, Mary was one of the altar workers. She used to help people pray though for the Baptism in the Holy Spirit. It seemed that every person she prayed with came through speaking in other tongues, as the Spirit gave them utterance. Some of the local townspeople did not like this, and were very upset with Mary for her success in this area. They threw rotten eggs at her, and tomatoes and other fruit and vegetables, and even attacked her physically for her ministry success. Even during her days at Bethel Bible School in New England she conducted many meetings throughout New England while she was still a single lady in Bible school. She, too, began to see some healings in her meetings after ministering alongside Maria Etter.

Mary Duncan Meets Harry Crandall

The year was 1914 when Mary was about to graduate from E.W. Kenyon's Bethel Bible School. Meanwhile, in Ledyard Connecticut, Stephen Carl Watrous (the grandfather of Cornelius B. Watrous, father of the author), who was a residential builder, learned of Mary Duncan's reputation as an evangelist. He was brother to Fred Watrous, pastor of Quakertown Church in Ledyard, Connecticut. So Steve and Fred Watrous invited her to come and speak at some meetings in the Mystic Connecticut and Ledyard, Connecticut area. So Mary answered that call, and began preaching in that beautiful coastal area of eastern Connecticut. Many attendees in those meetings received the baptism of the Holy Spirit, especially among the Quaker community made up of many families, including most notably the Watrous'es, Crouches, and Whipple's. Mary Duncan subsequently moved to the area and continued holding meetings. The Pentecostal message came to Connecticut mainly by way of these two people; Mary Duncan and Stephen Carl Watrous. The Quakertown Church in Ledyard which hosted Mary Duncan's meetings eventually became known as the Quakertown Assembly of God Church on Colonel Ledyard Highway in Ledyard.

(**Footnote:** Pastor Fred Watrous was the pastor of this Quakertown Church located on Colonel Ledyard Highway in Ledyard, Connecticut. Later Fred's son, Steve Watrous, along with his wife, Margit Watrous, pastored the church after that. This church is still in operation, and is now currently being pastored by Steve and Margit's son, Mark Watrous and his wife Jarrica Watrous. The church has recently had a name change to become Friendship Community Church. The relationships of the Crandall's and Watrous'es became intertwined and eventually several marriages took place between the families. Pastor Fred Watrous was uncle to Cornelius Watrous, who married Mary Duncan's second daughter, Mary Esther Crandall. Pastor Fred Watrous was also the father of Marge Watrous, who married Joseph Crandall, the third son of Mary Duncan Crandall. He also became a pastor of several congregations in his own right.)

Harry Willis Crandall

Mary Meets Harry

The following story was told by Ben Crandall concerning his mother's courtship and marriage to Willis Harry Crandall of Mystic: Among the converts in Mystic was Willis Harry Crandall, the man Mary was destined to marry. Harry had been born in Mystic on the William Crandall farm on Flanders Road (see photo on

28

page 32). Mary was impressed by this handsome young man, and Harry was absolutely fascinated by this fiery young woman evangelist. He was converted and baptized right away. Then he felt called to preach and began to speak and witness wherever he had an opportunity. Mary was a very private person when it came to some personal aspects of her life. Her romance with Harry was one of them. We do know, however, that they dated only a few times. Harry felt called to the ministry and now they would continue in evangelism together, she hoped and believed.

It was told that when Harry Crandall heard Mary preach, he made the decision right away that he would marry her someday, because he was greatly smitten and fascinated by this young woman named Mary. He even began predicting out loud that he would marry her and he began telling people that. And yes, he even told Mary that... finally, after the fact! But Mary was also very impressed by this handsome young man! After only a few dates they had a short courtship, lasting a few weeks. They were also close to the same age, Mary being one year older than Harry. She was 27 years old and Harry 26 on their wedding day.

The wedding was set for Sunday afternoon, May 26th 1915, in the Crandall's living room in Mystic. The farm had a huge apple orchard and lots of vegetables in the summer for food. Their marriage license can be seen in the photo on the page following the wedding photo, below.

**Newlyweds Harry Willis Crandall and
Mary Duncan Crandall at their wedding**

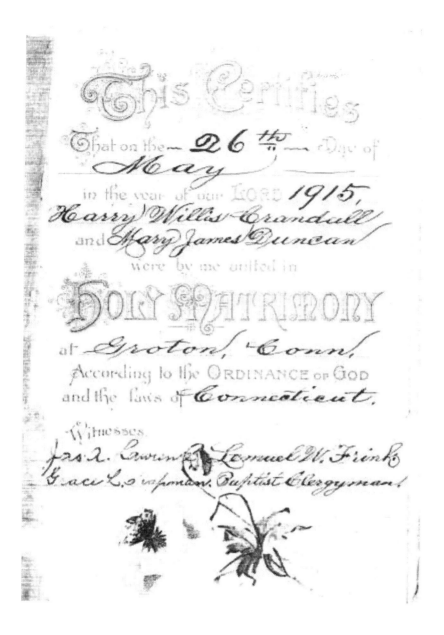

This Certifies

That on the 26th Day of May in the year of our Lord 1915, Harry Willis Crandall and Mary James Duncan were by me united in

HOLY MATRIMONY

at Groton, Conn, According to the ORDINANCE of GOD and the laws of Connecticut.

Witnesses.

Jas. X. Lawrence   Lemuel W. Frink

Grace L. _____ Baptist Clergyman

Harry Crandall and Mary Crandall's Marriage License

The William Crandall Farm House on Flanders Road

"Mary was a gorgeous bride! She had beautiful, thick red hair and her complexion was absolutely flawless, pure peaches and cream. Her eyes were as blue and clear and bright as the sky. Her posture was as straight as any cadet's, but that wasn't what made Mary the outstanding person she was. It was her soul that made her great - she was a true person, very strong in her convictions, dedication to God, family, and to the people she served. This was beyond life itself. Mary was true all the way, right down to her very bone. They married that day, and made their home in Connecticut." These were the words of her son, Ben Crandall!

Mary Duncan Crandall

Mary and Harry lived together in Connecticut and North Carolina for nine years. Four of their six children were born in Connecticut and the other two in North Carolina. Harry worked in a mechanic's shop off of highway 184 in Groton, Connecticut. He also worked in the boat yard in nearby Noank, Connecticut, as well. He always did very well wherever he worked. They held meetings in their home and around the area in other churches and homes. Because wherever Mary was there would always be a meeting... always!

Harry and Mary Crandall's family

Harry and Mary were blessed with the birth of their first child, Elizabeth Jane, in 1916 at Roseboro, North Carolina, while visiting with her family in the south. Next, Duncan was born in Ledyard in 1917, and then Mary Esther was born in Roseboro in 1918. Then the family returned north to Connecticut and the remainder of the children were born there: Douglas in 1919, Joseph in 1921, and then Benjamin was born in Old Mystic, Connecticut in 1925.

In spite of bearing children, Mary continued evangelizing throughout New England, in addition to holding many services in their home. It was a crowded, busy place. Annie (the sister closest to Mary's age) had a son named Henry. He moved in with the Crandall family in Connecticut when he was a teenager. He worked outside the home, but boarded with Mary's family. Harry's times away from home became more frequent as the years rolled by. Harry continued to try to support the family, but his support became less and less reliable.

Along the way, the family had a series of old rented houses they lived in which were in the general Mystic/Ledyard area. Moves were sometimes necessary because Mary did not have the rent money when the landlord required it of her. The exact addresses they lived in are not remembered today but no doubt the courthouse in Groton would have the birth certificates and they should show the addresses where the Crandall family was living when each child was born, because all the children were born at home in those days. One home was on Lambtown Road, and then another house that later burned down was on Quakertown Road. They also lived in an older home in Old Mystic when Benjamin was born. This home has been fully restored at great expense and is now a beautiful million dollar residence.

Finally, for their last residence in Connecticut, of all places to live, their family moved into a Quaker Meeting House for a period of time!

The next section contains a brief sketch on each of the Crandall children:

Elizabeth Jane Crandall was born in Roseboro, North Carolina in 1916, but the family still lived in Connecticut for a few more years. She moved back to Falcon, North Carolina in 1928, and graduated from Falcon High School in 1933. Jane was the first of the children to marry. She married Thurman Maxwell on January 6th, 1934. Of this union four children were born, Edna, Sheryl, Marilyn and Harold.

Elizabeth Jane Crandall

Duncan Crandall was born in Ledyard, Connecticut in 1917. He moved to Falcon, North Carolina, in 1928 and was graduated in 1934. He attended Holmes Bible College for two years and later graduated from Zion Bible Institute in 1944. He married Hazel Moone of Providence, Rhode Island, to whom were born five children: Paul, Dale, Nancy, Brenda and Elizabeth. They were divorced and he later married Joan Salany and had two daughters, Sherrilyn and Robin.

Duncan Crandall

Mary Esther Crandall was born November 2, 1918, in Falcon, North Carolina, but the family home was in Connecticut. She moved back to Falcon in 1928, and graduated from Falcon High School in 1935. She attended People's Bible School in Greensboro, North Carolina. She married Cornelius B. Watrous in 1948. To this union were born five children: Mary Edith, Steve, Marlene (your author), Barry and Debbie.

Mary Esther Crandall

Douglas Crandall was born in 1919 in Ledyard, Connecticut. (see photo on page 42) He attended Falcon, North Carolina schools until 1933. He died in November 1938 in a gravel pit accident while saving another man's life.

Joseph C. Crandall was born December 25, 1921, in Ledyard, Connecticut. He moved to Falcon, North Carolina in 1928, where he attended school through the ninth grade. He graduated from Zion Bible Institute in 1943. He also married Marjorie Watrous in 1943. This couple was blessed with twelve children: Elizabeth Jean, Margaret, Ann, Joseph Jr., Rosemary, Danny, Arlene, David, Sylvia, Philip, Esther and John.

Joseph Crandall and Benjamin Crandall

(A note here about Joseph: before he was born, the Lord told his mother Mary, that she was going to give birth to a son who would become a prophet in the last days.) Joseph Crandall pastored churches in Maine, Massachusetts, Long Island, Pennsylvania, Florida and Virginia, and was always active in evangelism and missions work. Joseph always had a decidedly prophetic gifting.

Benjamin Crandall was born in Old Mystic, Connecticut in 1925. He moved to Falcon in 1928, attending the Falcon schools from grade one through ten, then at 14 years of age he moved back to New London, CT and finished high school there. He graduated from Zion Bible Institute in 1945. He married Jeanne Bither of Houlton, Maine. This couple had two children, Douglas and Karen.

Benjamin Crandall

Benjamin was Assistant Pastor of Calvary Tabernacle beginning 1945, assisting Mary Crandall. In 1950 Ben became the Senior Pastor of Calvary Tabernacle of Brooklyn, New York, a dynamic Pentecostal church that grew to more than 2000 attending. Later he became President of Zion Bible Institute.

The four Crandall boys (l to r) Benjamin, Joseph, Douglas and Duncan

Benjamin was named after the Benjamin in the Bible, of course, but was given no middle name. Later, when Benjamin learned of this, he gave himself a first name, Nathan, because he was particularly fond of his uncle Nathan Duncan. After Benjamin was born, Mary began conducting evangelistic meetings in the Ledyard, Connecticut Town Hall for a number on months.

Because of the significance of Mary's blind sister Florence in the life of Mary and her children, it is fitting here to tell more about her and her role within the family framework. Ben explains if very well this way: "She couldn't see with her eyes but she could see with her heart and hands. She was the one who was able to give love most freely to her siblings and later to our family, loving us as if we were her own, while she lived with us and never married." Years later she would still type sweet letters to Mary Duncan's second daughter, Mary Esther, calling her, "baby lamb," and filling her in on all the family news and reminding her to please return back to Falcon as often as possible.

Each of Mary's children was loved and nurtured by Florence, especially Benjamin, the youngest. His older brothers teased him frequently and asked him '*WHEN* would he be moving upstairs with them?' and quit staying downstairs with "Aunt Florence?" Later, when Benjamin got a little older and was good and ready, he bounded up the stairs to bunk in with his older brothers, Duncan, Douglas, and Joseph!

The boys were always close to Mary's side of the Duncan family. Mary Esther Crandall often spent a lot of time in the south staying with Aunt Florence throughout the years. Sometimes Mary Esther would stay with her Aunt Florence for six months out of the year in Falcon, after she had graduated from high school and had become a young woman.

A Letter from Home

About this time a letter arrived from Mary Crandall's father, Henry Duncan. It gives a glimpse into life of this family in the year 1920. As of the date of the writing of the letter Henry is almost 76 and his wife Eliza Duncan is 72. It was posted from Roseboro, North Carolina on September 7, 1920. Spelling is as it appeared in the letter:

"Dear daughters Florence, Mary and the children, also Willis (Harry),

I am trying to write to you all one time more. I and your good mother received Mary's affectionate letter pm, and for her expressed opinion that we had been libral toward our children. I have done all I was able to do and more in one case than I should have done, and now I am now needing help but do not get it. If I had what is owing to me, I and your good mother would be in easy circumstances. I am not able to get eny work worth talking about. Some times I try to cut or brake a little wood for your ma to cook with but it hurts me for sevral days. So I am not able to do eny thing and I have to take the bed and rest for sevral days but thanks be to God I still am on mercy's side of the cross and I do continue to preay that I may so be restored to helth The Bible says it is good to be afflicted for when I am afflicted went not astray.

It is a hard matter to get a little work done. I have payed men to cut and hall wood for us and they promis every time we see them, but they keep away. Father have mercy on such caracters. I trust that God will take cear of us.

We do thank you all for your prears and good advice and we hope we may be speared yet meney days and that God may yet premitt us to do some good in his cause. I am impressed that I aught to preach and have meney initiations to go to churches and preach. I hope to be able to do to Roueau on 3rd Sunday. Will you all pray to that end.

We had a good meeting at Roseboro Baptist Church beginning on 2nd Sunday night of August. I and Ma went nearly every day but not at night. 20 was addressed, by letter and watcher of the church, 7 by Baptism. When I am able to go to church or Sunday School, I go. If not, then I stay at home and read or study the scriptures.

We want you to pray much for us. We do want to see you all and them sweet little children. Remember us very kindly to them and kiss them also for us.

We are glad indeed you have meney chickens and that your hoghs are so fine. We have not meney chicks and we have ony 3 hogs. They are doing nicely.

Well, Robadam Butter came to see us last Wednesday and spent some time with us. He seamed to enjoy himself very much and inquired of *you all and said he would be so glad to see you all. Our corn crop is rite good. I am done sowing the fodder. I only pulled about one achor and it hurts my rite arm and shoulder until now. My cotton crop I rented out. It has been injured by the drough but has rained for last few days and is looking better now.*

Well I must tell you that sister and William left this morning to go for 2 or 3 weeks. We will miss them. William has groad lots but he ought to be in school.

Your dear mother sends lots of love to you all and wants to see each of everyone of you. She says it would seam so good to have Florence with her a while that Mary could not spear her now on account of the dear little children. She prays for you all every day and night.

God bless you is our prears.

H.J. & E.J. Duncan

Harry abandons the family

In 1924 a major tragedy struck this young family. Their father Harry had loved the meetings, loved the Spirit and even felt called to preach on his own. He even conducted some meetings, or spoke in the meetings held by others. But their home was a crowded, busy place. It seemed that there was always a Duncan in town visiting, and with six children, the house was always buzzing with activity. Sometimes Harry might have felt there was no room for him in the crowd.

Harry went down south to Florida in the winter of 1924 to hold meetings with another minister there. He had gone on other trips to minister with a team, but this time things proved to be different. This time Harry never returned. That was in December, and Benjamin, the last child of this union, was born in February. Harry left two months before Benjamin was born. He would write letters back from Florida, and send some money for a short period of time along with these letters, but before long the letters completely stopped. It would be years before they heard from their father again. So Benjamin, Mary's youngest son, never really knew his father, Harry. Mary's sister, 'blind Aunt Florence' came to stay with their family and help Mary with the children just one month before Benjamin was born.

Years later it was learned that somewhere Harry had met a woman in the restaurant business. He divorced Mary and married this new woman at some point later. Benjamin did not see his father until after his brother Douglas was killed fourteen years later. At that point Harry came to see the family in Falcon. Ben was fourteen at the time his father arrived to see the family in North Carolina for his brother, Douglas' funeral.

Benjamin's Crandall perspective on Harry:

"My mother had this great attitude, which she passed down to her children. My mother always said, 'That is your father and you must respect your father.' So, I didn't hate him. It was my mother and Aunt Florence who taught us never to disrespect our mother or father, no matter what the circumstances."

1920's Living Conditions in Connecticut by Jane Crandall Maxwell

So another great tragedy encompassed Mary's life, being abandoned by her husband with six young children and no means of financial support. How could they go on, how could they pay the bills, find food or clothes for the children; who would provide for this household? Mary would again have to draw from her experience and faith in God's miraculous provision.

In Connecticut, the home the Crandall family occupied did not have electricity or running water. They used oil lamps. The wells were outside but there was a pump in their pantry. Washings were done using a washboard. Water was heated on the wood or coal stove and poured into the washtub. They lived very meagerly; Mary dressed quite simply with a single cameo brooch on her dress. If the children did have any extra money it would be used to purchase little items at the five and dime store for the house. They all slept in unheated bedrooms, but there was a stove in Mary's room.

46

Clothes were provided for the family from others who helped, and it appears from the pictures that were taken there was no sign of ragged clothes. While living in Ledyard there were ponds where the children ice-skated and swam. There were cranberry bogs and horses and men who cut ice in the winter. There was a barn full of hay next door to the Crandall's where the children spent many happy hours. They clearly made the best of their situation, no matter how desperate it might appear to be.

At school the children made Christmas tree decorations and they would help cut down a tree for Christmas Day. Marge (Watrous) Crandall's relatives, who were the Cheesbro family, always were active in bringing joy to the Crandall household at Christmas time. A friend, Mr. Lawrence, acted as Santa Claus on Christmas Eve. They brought toys to the family and invited them all over for Christmas dinner. According to Jane they had the prettiest Christmas trees ever.

The Crandall children always had many friends who were their classmates and neighbors who came over after school to play. There were plenty of chores to be done for the household, and the older children had to care for the younger ones. Mary Esther had to watch after Joe and Jane looked after little Ben. Mary had devotions with the children every day—always at bedtime and on Saturday mornings. Whenever Aunt Florence was staying with them she told Bible stories in the evenings, which the children loved!

Whenever there was a need in the family, Mary gathered together the children in prayer and asked God to supply the need. Mary was always known to be singing as she worked around the home. This family was dirt poor by any measure. But if Mary was ever despondent the children never knew about it. She always lived a life of victory! They never saw her cry because she was discouraged. And she never made a negative remark about the children's father.

Moving From House To House

There had never been the kind of financial provision that enabled the family to have stability. Along the way, the family had a series of old rented houses they lived in which were in the general Mystic/Ledyard Connecticut area. Moves were sometimes necessary because Mary did not have the rent money when the landlord required it of her.

The house in which Mary Crandall's youngest child, Benjamin, was born is still standing in Old Mystic. It was very rundown at one time, but as of today it has been very expensively restored and is a beautiful, million dollar residence, see photo below.

Daughter Jane's Miraculous Healing

While the Crandall family was still living in Ledyard, Jane became very sick. She was in the third grade and it was wintertime. The weather was very bad. Jane became so sick that her jaws locked up on her. Aunt Florence and Jane's mother Mary would take turns holding her because Jane couldn't lie down for several days. Finally, after she could lie down, she was confined to her bed.

Each week a group of ladies met at Mary's home for prayer. One evening they prayed for Jane's healing; while they were in prayer a knock came on the door. It was the health authorities and they brought a nurse along with them. "We hear that you have a sick girl here. May we see her?" "Certainly", replied Mary. The nurse took Jane's pulse, checked her all over, and was convinced that Jane was okay. The group left.

Jane got up out of bed immediately because God had healed her on the spot. At first she was experiencing weakness and had to learn to walk again. However, she returned to school in two weeks. God had done another miracle in the Crandall home. Note: Jane received a certificate from her school for the following school year noting that she had perfect attendance for the year of 1926. She was truly healed!

"God Will Provide" by Joseph Crandall

While the Crandalls were living in Old Mystic, CT, God provided a meal as follows:

"One day a black man came to the porch with a bag of groceries. Mary answered the door and the gentleman said, 'Would you cook these pork chops for me?' 'Yes', she replied. 'You sit here on the porch and I will do it for you.' Mary cooked the pork chops and brought them out for the gentleman. She looked on the porch but the man could not be found. Daughter Jane believed the man must have been an angel and God used him to provide a meal for the Crandall's that day."

In a small village like Old Mystic, Connecticut, everyone usually gets to know everything about everyone else. This village certainly was no exception. It soon became common knowledge that Mrs. Crandall was living in that old house with her six children and a blind sister. There was lots of free advice offered. Some folks were sincere friends and genuinely concerned. Others were almost hysterical. In fact, one lady said, "If this were happening to me, I'm afraid I would lose my mind." And she asked Mary if she was afraid of losing her mind. It is instructive to look back on Mary's answer to the woman, "My dear, this is no time for me to lose my mind; this is just the time I need it most, and why should I? I have the Lord!"

Others implored Mary to call the authorities and turn the children over to the state of Connecticut, saying "Now Mrs. Crandall, you know you can't just keep these children. How are you going to feed them? How are you, alone, ever going to put clothes on them all? And what are you going to do about the rent? You have no money – who is going to pay the rent for you? You have no choice; you will have to turn your children over to the state! It would take nothing less than a miracle to keep those children here". Mary's answer was always the same... she had the Lord! And she could pray. Man, oh man, could she pray! God had never failed her in the past, and she could see no reason He would fail her in the future.

She truly lived by the Word of God and prayer. Two of her favorite scriptures that became the foundation of her life were:

> "But my God shall supply all of your needs according
> to His riches in glory by Christ Jesus." - Philippians 4:19

> "Be anxious for nothing, but in everything by prayer and
> supplication with thanksgiving let your request be known
> unto God." - Philippians 4:6

Mary lived out these scriptures every day of her life. They were the source of her strength to carry on. They were her very foundation!

**Aunt Florence with Ben Crandall in Connecticut
before the family moved south**

The neighbors grew so concerned that at one point someone alerted the State of Connecticut Welfare Department that their father had deserted the family. The Welfare Department sent two agents out to visit Mary. They asked her if she had any regular support. She told them that God supplied all her needs and that His provision was very regular—everyday in fact. They informed her that her concept of support didn't meet the requirements of the Welfare Department. They left, but soon returned with a station wagon to take all of the children away to be placed in foster homes.

Now Mary, being a red-haired, Holy Ghost woman, was not about to turn her children over to the Welfare Department. She told them God would continue to supply their needs... that she would raise her own children and that they would all grow up to preach the Gospel. Shortly after, the Sheriff served papers on Mary to appear in court. Mary and the family spent much time in prayer before the court appearance.

The day arrived for her to go to court and make her defense. When told to take the witness stand and to swear to tell the truth, she told the Judge she could not swear, because the Bible says, "Swear not." At that moment the power of the Holy Ghost came upon her and she began to testify to all the supernatural provisions of the Lord, not only for material needs, like the family's food and clothing, but for the healing of their bodies too. There wasn't a dry eye in the courtroom. When Mary sat down the judge made this decision, "I am delivering these children back to their mother. It is for them a privilege and a great honor to be raised by a mother with such great faith and power. Case dismissed!"

Circumstances had closed Mary in with God. She was deserted by Harry and left with six small children alone, far from home and family. Many times the children would head off to school without any lunch, but always, without fail, God would supply before lunchtime. From time to time the local authorities came to check upon the Crandall family unannounced to see if they had groceries...because the family had been told, "If we ever find the pantry bare we will take your children." However, people often brought groceries to the family just prior to the authorities coming to check on them or just prior to mealtime. The children never went hungry, God always provided. For example, He provided with the help of two Quaker sisters called Aunt Carrie and Aunt Phoebe (aunt by courtesy). They would hook up their horse and buggy and drive over to see the family... what welcome guests they were, and such wonderfully good people! They always brought full meals and more with them for each visit.

During her years of ministry, whenever Mary returned home from speaking and teaching she might bring home a little money from the offerings. She may also have been given some chickens, corn, rice, or other produce, etc. Sometimes people gave her canned vegetables, or even pork. People gave of what they had to give in those days. More than likely it may not have been much, but it did help to sustain them and for that they were very grateful.

On one occasion the family found itself snowed in and stranded by a blizzard that was so bad it took days before the plows could open the roads. The snowdrifts covered the windows and some were so high they reached the roof. During this time, the family's supply of wood was being used up. There was no phone and no way to get help. Mary felt it was time to pray, so the family all prayed together. The oldest son, Duncan, came in from his room and said God told him that a supply of wood would come before the last piece of wood was consumed. Aunt Florence, who was staying with the family at the time, worried to herself that Duncan's faith would be shattered. Attempting to prepare him for a disappointment she said, "You poor boy, there is no way that anyone could get wood here today, and no one even knows that we are out of wood."

As the fire burned low and Aunt Florence was forced to place the last stick of wood on the fire, suddenly they heard a truck pulling into the driveway. There was a knock at the door and to Aunt Florence's delight, there stood a burly farmer and his son. He had a bewildered look on his face. He explained, "I went out to milk my cows and I heard a voice, loud and clear, tell me that the family on the hill needs wood. I thought I was tired and overworked and my mind was playing tricks on me. But I heard it again. I told myself, if I hear that voice once more, I'll go and carry wood to that family. The voice spoke again, so my son and I put chains on the truck and filled it up with wood." "Lady," he said, "do you need this wood?" Mary told him that our last piece of wood was already on the fire. God does hear and answer prayer! Miracles like this occurred continually during the family's stay in Connecticut. God never failed to meet even the smallest need.

Religious Persecution in Ledyard Connecticut by Jane Crandall

When Mary was preaching at the Ledyard Town Hall, In Connecticut, there were some people in town who rebelled against them and their message. During one revival that was going on there, Mary's children were sitting, as usual, on the front seats of the hall. It was Jane's place to watch over little Benjamin who sat next to her.

The service opened with songs and worship and then the service was grossly interrupted. Tomatoes were thrown in through the windows first. Next came a lighted gas lantern and it landed right in front of Jane and Ben. God was watching over them, because instead of igniting further or exploding, the flames were extinguished.

These were desperate times for the family. Mary had no reliable income and her support, when she had some, came from the family in the south. What would they do, where would they turn? Life had taken a very bitter turn for this close family in New England. It seemed they were painted into a corner with no place to turn. How could Mary continue her ministry activities and also care for the children?

Possible boarding school plan is rejected:

Mary knew a woman named Sister Gibson from British Guiana. She knew her from the conferences and meetings they both attended. Sister Gibson had a children's home (boarding school), where missionary families left their children, when the parents left for missions work in countries not suitable for their children to live in. In her desperation, Mary had discussed with Sister Gibson the possibility of leaving the children in the home while she ministered from place to place. She had talked with her son, Duncan, and daughter, Jane, about this possibility before she felt the Lord told her to move south to Dunn North Carolina with her entire family.

Mary's dream to move south

But this plan was set aside when Mary heard the Lord tell her to move the family south. Mary's relatives in North Carolina got together and sent her money to move down south nearer to them. This is how that all happened:

In 1927, while Mary and her six children were living in Connecticut, God gave her a dream. She dreamed that she was very busily engaged in packing her things and moving to North Carolina with the children. In the dream she almost missed the train. It was as if God was saying, "You must hurry. Don't be slow. The economy is going to get worse and you must hasten." Nobody knew at that time that the Great Depression was right around the corner... beginning in 1929 and 1930. Mary knew this was a word from the Lord, and she did not hesitate to pack and help the children be ready. And it actually did happen that they almost missed the train.

Mary corresponded with Aunt Florence and her family in the South to let them know of the tremendous struggle the family was having making a living in Connecticut. The Duncan family in the South sent money for them to move back home to North Carolina by train. Aunt Florence came north to help the family in the moving process. So, Mary took some of the children on the train with her, while Aunt Florence took the rest. When they moved south, the family first settled in Dunn, North Carolina, in 1928 before the youngest, Benjamin, turned three years old.

Mary Duncan Crandall (on the right) and Aunt Florence Duncan

When Mary returned to NC with her brood, she "picked up where she left off." The people there who had helped support her while she was in Holmes and Bethel Bible Schools now asked her to become their pastor when she returned to the area. Mary prayerfully agreed. She helped to get the first Pentecostal Assembly in Dunn, NC organized and started! But, the next fifteen years, during the Great Depression, could well be described as a constantly recurring nightmare. Utter poverty – with six destitute children and one of the family a cripple. The children lived part of the time with Aunt Florence, while Mary conducted meetings. But her spirit was not broken. She had a mighty God and her trust in Him would never be shaken and the family would never be forsaken.

Aunt Florence, mother's sister who was blind, was the one who helped Mary with the daily care of the family. She had a good education. Aunt Florence graduated from a high school for the blind in the capital of Raleigh, North Carolina. She lived at the school during the school year and came back home to the family farm in the summers. Afterwards, Florence had represented the state of North Carolina School for the Blind and had the honor of speaking all over the state. She traveled by train with the help of Boy Scouts who received her and got her to the next location where she would speak. The blind association used her for some length of time in this manner and gave her a very small pension, which was something quite special for those days.

The Crandall family was very close-knit and there was a lot of joy, laughter and a great rapport with each other in the home. They were very tight and supportive of each other. Each person had specific duties that were vital to day-to-day living, just in order to make it. Mary Esther cut all the hair in the family. Everyone worked and many of the older children worked in the cotton fields, and whatever money they brought in was given toward the family needs.

One time Douglas and Ben were sawing logs and getting paid just a couple of pennies per log. They worked hard just to get fifteen or twenty cents for the day's work. They were sawing great big trees down and then took their money home. According to Ben, when they returned home, their Mother said, "What we really need is a can of salmon!" So they went down to the store and bought the salmon with all the money they had earned. No one thought anything about keeping the money for themselves in those days. They all lived together and whatever one had they all shared together.

In Dunn, North Carolina when Benjamin was a toddler and still on the bottle, he came down with colitis. Dr. Stacey Duncan, Mary's nephew, took Ben to the Rex Hospital in North Carolina. On the way, Ben's pulse stopped twice. Dr. Duncan stopped the car and cared for him. "Ben died twice on the way to the hospital" he recounted.

Mary sat in the hospital with him and prayed. Ben turned totally blue, but Mary kept praying and God brought him out of this illness. There was a terrible epidemic at this time and most of the other children who had been brought to the hospital were carried away dead. But Ben was healed and recovered completely.

Jane's tonsillitis Story and Mary Esther's dream

Jane was twelve years old and in the fifth grade at school in 1928 when she became ill. Her tonsils became very inflamed. The county nurse checked each student periodically. Several students needed to have their tonsils removed. A clinic had been set up over Mr. Hood's Drug Store in Dunn, NC for the removal of tonsils. An appointment was set for Jane to go to the clinic to have this operation.

Meanwhile, Mary Esther, who was ten years old at the time, had a dream. She woke up crying and said, "Jane, you cannot go and have your tonsils out because they will cut a vein and you will bleed to death." But Jane was scheduled to be there at 9 o'clock that morning.

Mary held off taking her daughter Jane, but about noontime, Mary and Jane walked downtown. By the drug store was a luncheonette, and Dr. Butler, Mary's nephew, was eating there and saw them walk by. He knocked on the window and beckoned for them to come in. Mary was still hesitant about having the operation done, and Dr. Butler said, "Why not have them removed? All the students are doing okay."

Jane and her mother Mary walked into the drug store and she again expressed doubt that Jane should go through with the operation. Mr. Hood said, "Why should you be afraid? Everyone's okay." So Mary and

Jane ascended the stairs and the nurse took Jane in to have the operation performed. They did remove the tonsils, and put Jane down on a bed in a nearby room. The nurse kept checking on Jane, but suddenly Mary noticed blood and discovered that Jane was bleeding very badly. They took Jane back into the operation room and packed gauze into her mouth. They couldn't give her any more anesthesia.

Jane was facing the wall, and she called, "Turn me over." When they tried to move Jane, she began hemorrhaging. All the packing came out. They returned her to the operating room. And still with no anesthesia, they stitched up the incision. They warned her not to move or else she might die.

Jane had to remain there all night. They had a very hard time getting the bleeding to stop. Mary stayed with her. The next day, Mary took her home "on a pillow." Jane recovered very slowly. She stated that she suffered every time she had a cold. The scar tissue remained. Mary Esther's dream had been a warning from the Lord. But He is faithful and He protected Jane's life on that occasion.

Living in Dunn, NC

When they moved from Connecticut, the family first moved to a small town named Dunn. At first the house in Dunn, North Carolina seemed to work our quite well. The house was by the railroad tracks… How lonesome and sad it would make the children feel when the train whistle would blow far off in the distance late at night. Then… the same story that the family had been through so many times was repeated. Mary could not afford the rent, so with six growing children and a blind aunt, the small house in Dunn just wasn't the place for them any longer. (By this time they had moved so many times that it had almost become a lifestyle. The young family had lived in four houses in Connecticut and now was moving to a second home in North Carolina.)

It was New Years Eve, and Mary felt the burden of it all. They had to move, but where to this time? And what with? Where could they go? Mary went to church that night, not to see anyone or to hear anyone, she went to meet God. And, as she would say, "to pray through." By that expression she meant praying until she got a clear answer from God. And in this case she felt she had no choice - she just had to have an answer! She was kneeling at the altar with tears trickling down her cheeks, her face turned heavenward, as out of her broken heart she sought God for a place for the family to live. This is the way Mary told the story... "It was unusually quiet at that moment, just before midnight. And as the old year was about to go out and the New Year come in, God spoke to me. There were just these three words that came to me; however, they came with great assurance... "I have undertaken". That was all, but that was enough. The meeting ended and everyone went home. Everything was the same. The pressure was still on. The family still had to vacate the house. Outwardly nothing improved, but deep inside she had peace. Those words were still there. "I have undertaken! I have undertaken!"

Mary was in peace as a few days passed, and then she received a letter from her brother John. It was brief and went something like this.... "Dear Mary, I have bought and paid for the house in Falcon. It is yours. Move in! Love, John." The house mentioned was a vacant house in a small town nearby that had casually been mentioned in a recent visit. Needless to say, the family moved at once. Ben states, "What joy! We didn't move again from the house in Falcon until I was a young man when it was years later, and our family would move north once again. The house in Falcon that the Lord had given us was more than just a house – it truly became OUR HOME!" (The first secure home the family had ever occupied).

While Mary was busy with her growing family, Mary's brother, John Duncan, the youngest brother, had gone on to school, and then continued to seminary and became a Baptist minister. He was a wonderful man who cared for his family and helped his siblings whenever possible throughout his lifetime.

It was this brother, John, who had helped Mary financially with her family's train expense and helped get them established in North Carolina. Their first house had been in Dunn, North Carolina, and then later came a move to Falcon, North Carolina, into a larger home that John had bought for them. He never deeded it over to Mary, but paid the taxes on the house as long as she needed his help.

Mary's brothers and sisters also helped furnish this home for them. During the years previously, when they were living in the north in Connecticut, it was Mary's brother John, who had helped them from time to time by paying some of the rent for their home.

Uncle John kept the house paid until Aunt Florence died and all of his sisters were finished living there, and then he sold it. He sold the house to someone who never paid him and then later the house burned to the ground, which is sad to say...

They were lean times; there was never enough money to go around. Shortages were common. Benjamin remembers going to neighbors to borrow necessities: "Sometime I would have to ask for help from our neighbors. Time after time I was sent to the neighbors to say, 'Aunt Florence wants to know if we could possibly have a glass of milk, that is, if you have enough and if you can spare it..' Most of the time our neighbors were marvelous, but there were times when they would stare straight at me and, saying nothing, reach reluctantly for the glass. I would hang my head and stare at the cracks in the floor. I got the message. My tender spirit had been crushed like a young bird under a mule's hoof."

Picking Cotton

It was about this time that Jane was old enough to begin to help chop cotton in the early spring, and then later, when it was ripe, she picked it. Duncan also helped in this endeavor, as did the other children as they became older. Cotton was a very lucrative crop in the south in those days. Cotton was once so costly in Europe that only the royalty could afford to buy the fabric. There are only limited geographic areas of the world where cotton can be grown commercially. But the white, fluffy fleece that it provides goes from the fields to the mills and then to almost every part of the globe where it serves a greater number of useful purposes than any other plant fiber. Settlers of the frontier in the south soon learned that this land was ideal to grow cotton. The cotton belt of North America now extends from southwest Virginia south to Florida and west to Texas. It was the most profitable crop available to farmers in the south in the 1800s. So it should be no surprise to find Mary's family busily engaged in the cotton growing process. After early planting, the process of chopping cotton in the spring was necessary to thin out the plants to bring maximum cotton production. Picking cotton in the fall was hot and painful, as the plants have sharp pointed edges around the cotton boll. But, it was honest work, and it provided a little bit of needed income.

When the children would work in the cotton fields, the money they earned went to the family, to help put basic food on the table along with other needed items. Sometimes there was a special treat and that was reserved for birthdays, a birthday cake, as there wasn't enough money for gifts. A treat might even be considered milk toast with sugar on it for the entire family.

The house that Uncle John gave to the family in Falcon when they returned south was situated on an acre of land. Here the family planted a big garden. The children and Aunt Florence would help Mary plant it. It was big and beautiful! They had a model garden and people would come by just to look at it, because it was so well done and carefully maintained. It had all kinds of fruits and vegetables and lots of flowers! Mary worked in it whenever she was home. They raised potatoes, tomatoes, and all kinds of vegetables. Then they canned the vegetables for use in the winter. They seemed always to have plenty of canned vegetables for the whole winter. (Mary's son Joseph took after his mother and continued this tradition with a big, beautiful organic garden every year himself.)

They also raised chickens, and there were one or two pigs being fed all the time. Chickens and pigs gave them the meat that was needed to go with the vegetables. There was no refrigeration down south in those days, so they had to put up salt pork to preserve the pork for a period of time, or it would quickly spoil. It was placed in a box with salt to keep it. Most Sundays the family enjoyed a chicken dinner together. That was a real treat! They would buy a bunch of baby chicks, about 50 of them, for $2.00. They raised them and ate them when they became full grown. It was a very affordable way to have meat! One of the kids would go out and catch a chicken, and then they would kill it, pluck it, and cook it up for dinner. Now that was really fresh chicken!

The children all worked in the summertime, and were hired to work mostly on farms. They would pick cotton to help purchase their own clothing. One time while Ben was working with his brother Douglas on a farm, they were earning 45 cents a day. They worked 12 hour days in a corn field chopping weeds out of the rows. They worked from 7 in the morning to 7 at night. One day, about ten in the morning, they grew so tired that they sat down in the shade of a row of corn and the farm owner saw them and fired them on the spot. Ben was about eleven or twelve years old by then.

They children never forgot the ice cold water from the well on the farm! When given a break in mid-morning and mid-afternoon they got to get a drink from that well water...it tasted so good, they were so thirsty. Ben said, "Douglas would let everyone else drink first. He then said, 'when I drink I don't want anyone telling me to hurry' so he could have the next turn. He wanted to drink until he was satisfied, so he always went last."

Whatever was earned was part of the family's finances. When one would earn a sum of money and come home, my Aunt Florence would say, "We need some salmon and bread." Then the children would run down to the store and buy it for her. When they came home with it she made salmon cakes for dinner. A loaf of bread and a can of salmon and some eggs (and maybe a little onion) would make salmon cakes for the entire family. It was good, everyone liked it, and they ate it frequently. A can of salmon cost less than 10 cents.

Persecution for Her Lord

Mary continued her evangelistic work in the Dunn/Falcon area as she was also pastor of the local Pentecostal church. But evangelism sometimes comes with a price. During one service in the big Pentecostal Tabernacle at Falcon, NC, Mary was praying with a number of people at the altar, several of which had been experiencing the gift of the Holy Spirit upon their lives. Most of the folks had left for home but a few were still at the altar or just sitting in their seats quietly.

Suddenly a lady came forward who had been in the restroom and began to

63

attack Mary. She jumped on Mary, pushed her over, began to beat her on the head, pulling at her hair, and beat upon her face until it started to bleed. By this time other people came around to Mary and pulled off this attacker. It was obvious to all she had demon spirits operating in her life.

Apples don't fall far from the tree. So it came to pass, during this time, that Mary Esther, who was still a young single woman, began to travel and speak at various churches. She experienced tremendous success winning souls. So Mary Esther began to go to many tent meetings and warehouses throughout the North Carolina area, speaking in towns such as Turkey, Warsaw, Salemburg, Roseboro, and many others.

Joseph's angel visitation

Youngest son Joseph has an angelic visitor: At age sixteen, an angel appeared in Joseph's bedroom and came through the ceiling, and stood near his bed. "He was very close – I could have touched him," Joseph states. Joseph saw the angel very distinctly as the angel spoke and said that he had been sent with five seeds to give to Joseph. He told this young man that he was to plant these seeds in his lifetime, in four different places: the mountains, the seashore, in the great valley, and in the Great Plains. The angel further told him not to dig a hole in the sand but to go and plant as the angel had commanded. It is interesting to note that these are the places in which Joseph planted churches:

> Plains – Coudersport PA
> Seashore – Sarasota, FL
> Mountains- Colorado Springs, CO
> Valley – Rocky Mount, VA

In each place God moved mightily and Joe founded a church, and God also richly provided the increase as Joseph obeyed the angel's instructions.

The whole family together...Front row: Benjamin, Joseph, Douglas, Duncan. Second row: Mary Esther, Jane, Mary Duncan Crandall and Florence Duncan.

Son Douglas Crandall has a clubfoot operation

Mary's second son, Douglas, lived his entire life till he was a teen with one foot turned inward. It didn't seem to stop his indomitable spirit, as he loved to be involved with everyone. When Douglas was about fourteen years of age, he was taken to South Carolina to have his foot operated on at the Shriner's Hospital there. Doctor Jim Butler, Mary's nephew, arranged for the surgery. The surgery was a success and Douglas found freedom and relief from that condition.   Douglas was nicknamed, "Sunshine" by Mary Esther, Jane and the others in the home as he had such a sunny personality! About the same time Joseph was twelve years and developed cataracts. That is extremely young to have cataracts! So Mary prayed for him and he was healed immediately!

The family suffers loss again, by Ben Crandall

"But, the most devastating family tragedy of all was just around the corner, about to strike the home like a gigantic bolt of lightning, shattering everything in its path. I shall never forget it; it all comes back to me now just as though it happened only last night. December 2, 1938 – when I came home the front door was open - I ran through the hall calling for Mother but no one answered. I went into the dining room where we stayed most of the time when it was chilly - it was the only room that had a stove in it. As I swung the door open I started to call, "Ma," but suddenly froze. My eyes moved slowly around the room - Aunt Florence was crying, her handkerchief drenched, her eyes twitching. (She was blind, and crying affected her eyes differently.) In fact, everyone was crying, but Mother's crying affected me most. She was crying, not hysterically, but from a completely broken heart. Her sobs moved me to the absolute depths of my being. She looked so pathetic as she took her hands from her tear-stained face; the sight pierced me like a knife. Finally I mustered the courage to speak, my voice trembling with apprehension, "What has happened?" Duncan pushed two telegrams across the table to me. The first one read, "Your son Douglas seriously injured at work." The second read, "Your son Douglas is dead!" We were stunned - like someone had hit us with a hammer!

"It just didn't seem possible - he had never been sick in his life. It was true that he had had a club foot, but that was straightened now and there wasn't anyone as much alive as he was. He made more noise than anyone! He was the most daring, the strongest, the best ballplayer - and now he was dead - two thousand miles away, near the Mexican border. The next five days were some of the longest of my life as we waited for his body to arrive by rail, all the way from Texas. How lonely and sad - late at night the train whistle would moan far off in the distance, and faintly you could hear the wheels pounding the steel tracks with the rhythm that only a train has. I wondered if he was on that train, alone, in some cold box-car, lying in his coffin and jostling back and forth, on his last ride home.

"For the first time, death had come to our family and with cruel hands had snatched away one of our loved ones. Ben recounts that the wound that was opened in Mother's heart that day never really healed. Years later his name could not be mentioned without tears coming to her eyes. Through it all I never once heard Mother question God. Her faith in Him never wavered - she never doubted His love or questioned His judgments. She served Him on the mountain peaks and in the valleys ... when the skies were bright and cheerful ... and when the heavens raged with their wildest storms. Those mighty chains of love that bound her heart to the heart of God were never broken."

Harry Willis Crandall comes to visit his family in Falcon.

Harry was told that his son Douglas, who was a minor, was working in a gravel yard in High Delco, Texas and pushed his co-worker out of the way at the very moment a large boulder was about to topple over on him. Just as he pushed him out of the way the boulder fell on Douglas and crushed him instead. So Harry made his way to Falcon, North Carolina, his first visit with the family since he abandoned them in Connecticut.

Harry's arrival - as told by Mary Esther who was then 20 years old

Mary Esther was chuckling over the following event (Harry Crandall coming to see them after being gone all those years) as she told the story to her daughter Marlene. "My father, Harry, showed up at the door looking like 'Dapper Dan,' in his nice suit and tie, and Mom was in the kitchen looking very large and round with her apron on and flour all over herself as she came to see who was at the door. Mary Esther said to herself, 'I knew right then and there that no relationship would ever work out between the two of them!'"

Years later Benjamin once asked, "Mother, didn't you ever get discouraged and feel like giving up?" She reflected for a moment and then, said, "Yes, Ben, but only once. I had been battling and battling, praying and praying. Things just didn't improve, and one day a desperate depression swept over my soul that lasted three days. I went into the woods and cried and cried. I was terribly tempted to give up - the devil kept talking to me, telling me it was no use, telling me to give up, it just wasn't worth it. I realized I was fighting for my very life as well as the lives of my children. For three days I prayed and sought God with all my heart and with every ounce of my strength. At the end of three days I had won and while I have had a lot of trials since then, I have never again been tempted with discouragement like that."

Mary's medicine for evangelizing seemed a bit strong, but she realized the patient's disease was a sure killer and she wouldn't take any chances. Her method brought remarkable results, although some who would not be helped reacted violently to it. However, this never bothered Mother in the least. She knew what she was doing and kept right on witnessing and praying for people - on the train, in the station, on the sidewalks, in the stores, on the bus, out of the subways, in elevators, in halls, doctors' offices, jails, hospitals, cars – and everywhere else one could possibly imagine - weddings, funerals, religious services and non-religious services. It was not always easy to be in her company, for few people's courage matched hers, even though her family loved her dearly and believed in what she was saying.

Everybody who came to her house she witnessed to, there were NO exceptions. Nobody would escape her witnessing to them. She always had tracts with her; she was always witnessing. She never let an opportunity pass. That vision had marked her life forever: she would never be the same. She was driven to tell them they needed God so they can flee the wrath to come in Hell's eternal flames.

Mary continued her evangelistic work even in the tough times. They had tremendous meetings wherever they would go. Mary scheduled meetings mornings and evenings while Aunt Florence watched over the children. There were many tobacco houses or warehouses where the tobacco would dry just after harvest season. When the leaves had cured, the warehouses were emptied and kept clean until tobacco picking time the next year. There were, therefore, many sizeable warehouses that could be used for evangelistic meetings. It was those buildings where many of

Mary's meetings were held all across North and South Carolina. Mary "lived in the Holy Spirit'; God directed her coming in and directed her going out.

Camp meetings in Falcon, North Carolina

When the Pentecostal Holiness camp meetings came every summer at the end of August in Falcon, North Carolina, many people would stay in the home with the family. The children had to give up their bedrooms and sleep on the floor. Mary enjoyed those camp meetings so much! Many of her friends that she knew from her travels would come to those meetings. All the local families made room for their friends and all the children slept on the floor, wherever they could, during those meetings. Mary's brother David and his wife Addie came to the meetings and would stay with them. He would get the shakes during those meetings until he couldn't hold a cup of coffee without shaking all the coffee out of the cup! Children did not forget things like that...

The meetings grew throughout the ten days of meetings until there were 5,000 people in the last meeting on the last Sunday of the camp. The governor of the state of NC came to speak at the camp meetings several of those years. He was invited to come by Mr. Culbraith who owned and directed the camp meetings.

Mary Crandall really loved the prayer meetings during camp meeting days. They had a sunrise prayer meeting. Hundreds of people gathered in prayer as the sun arose on those campgrounds. In the dormitory buildings they put a little straw or hay down and spread a blanket on it and that was the mattress. It was terribly hot and humid in August in the south, but they were accustomed to the conditions and were happy to be there. Some of the people were well to do people, but they were still happy to be at camp meeting. Some of the greatest preachers from across the country would be speaking at those meetings. Some meetings were about missions and the missionaries would come in, and others would be about evangelism and great evangelists would speak. It was the greatest camp meeting ever in the south in those days! There was just nothing like it, according to Ben.

J. A. Culbreth and the Pentecostal Holiness Camp meetings

Mr. Culbreth donated the land for the camp meetings, and donated the land for the church. He built an orphanage and donated the land and the money to build it. He operated the Falcon orphanage, wrote the senior quarterly for the Pentecostal Holiness denomination and was a real leader in the denomination. He donated the land for the school, too, and he paid the teachers with his own money. Some of Mary's children went to the school free of charge. He was one 'great man,' affecting his generation mightily for the kingdom of God! He came from a wealthy family and gave everything he had to God. His wife was a musician, who trained the orphanage girls' choir and the church choir. The choir traveled to raise money for the orphanage. Mr. Culbreth ran the camp meeting. It was operated for the Pentecostal Holiness denomination, but they did not run it. Mr. Culbreth ran it himself. It was more of a Pentecostal Camp Meeting than it was a 'Pentecostal Holiness' denominational camp meeting.

Later the state took control of the school but they still asked Mr. Culbreth to be in charge of it. The state paid the teachers so they could keep the doors open. Later when he retired, the state moved the school.

It was common in those days to see people slain in the Spirit (a term describing the effect of becoming overcome by the power of the Holy Spirit and passing unconscious under His presence). It seemed to be more common in those days than it is today. There were many manifestations of the Holy Spirit prevalent in those meetings. People seeing visions, prophesying, and speaking in tongues were common manifestations in those meetings of that day. When there were public tongues then there was an interpretation of those utterances so the people could understand the message being spoken.

The meetings became so large that the speakers had to begin to use microphones in those days. Microphones then were as large as a dinner plate, and were stationary. The sound quality was poor and the crowds were large. The amplifiers were of poor sound quality but were the best available at the time. In the very large gatherings there were no public tongues and interpretations other than from the platform due to the inability to hear people from the audience. There were no fans to blow the air around and cool the people off. There were large doors and big windows on the sides of the auditorium to allow the wind to come into the sanctuary, with wire mesh on the windows to keep the birds out. It was a nice looking, large brick building.

Falcon, North Carolina was a strategic site for the Pentecostal movement in the young country. It was there that several denominations and groups of churches came together and merged into what is now known as the Pentecostal Holiness Denomination. Representatives from two regional denominations, the Pentecostal Holiness Church of North Carolina and the Fire-Baptized Holiness Church, met in April of 1910 for two days to forge a "Basis of Union". That was taken back to leaders of both groups and considered by all the churches in both denominations for the next nine months. Then the group reconvened, and the new union of churches was given the name of 'The Pentecostal Holiness Church.' The meeting for consolidation was convened in the octagon-shaped building on the Falcon Campgrounds January 31, 1911. Later, churches affiliated with the Tabernacle Pentecostal Church and The Greenville Church joined the denomination, as well.

Mary Continues Holding Meetings

Mary was a prayer warrior and an exhorter. But she was an evangelist as well. She would hold meetings for weeks at a time. She would often bring a prophetic word as well. God showed Mary many things in the Spirit realm. Sometimes the meetings were in a brush arbor, other times they were in houses or held in churches. Wherever the doors for ministry were opened she would walk in. Sometimes she would be gone two or three weeks in a row. With Aunt Florence at the house the children always had parenting and structure within the home. One of the mothers would always be home.

The reader should understand by now that everything Mary did was from a revelation of the Holy Spirit. She would hear His voice and just go and do what she heard. She did not have any money to go do these things, but she prayed and asked God, "If you want me to go then you will have to bring me the money to do it". Then all the money came in and away she went…

The Children are Growing Up

By the early 1930's Mary's children were growing up. The first sure sign came when Jane Crandall decided to marry Thurman Maxwell, even though she was still quite young. Jane Duncan and Thurman Maxwell were married on January 6th 1934. Harry, her father, wrote a beautiful letter to Jane at this time and sent a wedding gift of silver to the newly married couple which meant so much to them. Thurman had a job as a crane operator in North Carolina. Later he moved to Connecticut and worked as a crane operator at Electric Boat Division of United Technologies Corp. in New London. Much later, he and Jane went to Hong Kong as missionaries.

Time to go back up north

One day while Mary was in prayer in Falcon, the Holy Spirit told her that she would be leaving the area. At this time, Jane and Thurman were living in Portsmouth, Virginia, where Thurman had a Civil Service job at the military base. Mary Esther was in Bible School in Greensboro, North Carolina. At that time Harry Crandall came by Jane's house for a visit. It was the first time that her father had visited her home in North Carolina.

About that time Thurman's job was terminated and they were wondering and praying about what to do next. Harry encouraged the children to move to Connecticut and said that he could help them find a job at the submarine base there. So Harry, Thurman, and Mary Esther went north to

Connecticut, after putting their personal belongings in storage. Harry stayed about a month in Connecticut before moving on.

Jane stayed in North Carolina arranging their personal belongings and preparing to move their young family to Connecticut as soon as possible. On Sept 1, 1939 Jane and their children joined Thurman in New London, Connecticut. They had rented a small apartment over the church that Thurman and Mary Esther were attending. They also helped out in this Full Gospel Church that was holding services below their apartment in New London.

In November, God showed Mary Crandall that she was also to join Mary Esther and Jane in New London. She came in December and helped out in the ministry there at the Full Gospel Church. And in January, the congregation voted Mary Crandall in as their full–time pastor.

In May 1940 this notice was written in the FAITH NEWSLETTER:
"Having been without a Pastor for some time, during which, Brother Karterude ably assisted in this capacity and held the Assembly together. The church felt led to call Sister Mary Crandall, who has long been active in the work of God, as their Pastor. She, together with her talented daughter, Mary Esther, have been ministering to the sick and carrying on the work in New London for the glory of God. "

It was said, "We feel confident that God's blessings rests upon the Assembly in New London and that He will continue to work in their midst and bring others in as they hold together in prayer and work unitedly for that purpose." The Maxwell's and Mary Esther continued to help the church to grow and prosper alongside Mother Crandall. Soon, the rest of the siblings (except for Ben) went north also, following in her footsteps.

The family reunited in Connecticut

Benjamin had not yet been able to travel to Connecticut to be with his family. He stayed behind, living in North Carolina with Aunt Florence. Finally, Mary could see that it was time for Benjamin to join the rest of his family. So Aunt Florence gave Benjamin the money to travel north to Connecticut and join his mother when he was 14 years old. The bus station sold Ben a ticket to go non-stop from Dunn, North Carolina to New London, Connecticut. But when he got to New York the bus line actually stopped there, and wasn't completing the trip as Ben had planned. However, the Lord took care of him.

Ben arrived about midnight into New York City with no money and he was sound asleep when the bus came to the station. Everyone else had already gotten off and the bus was pulled into the garage. When Ben awoke, the driver was standing there beside him. Ben found himself in New York City with no way to get to New London, Connecticut. After explaining his situation to the driver, the driver begins telling Ben where he needs to go next. "Here's what you gotta do..." he says! He was going to help Ben, and he told him to go where he says to go and make no mistakes! So God had mercy on him and the driver told him to go to the Greyhound Bus Station and see if they would honor the ticket to continue his trip to New London. And sure enough, the bus line did take it and he was able to continue his trip to Connecticut to be with Mary and the rest of the family!

Mary's Diary

Mary wrote in a small, black diary that has these words on the cover: "Belongs to Mary Crandall" and includes her name and address, as follows:

Mary D. Crandall
11 Pearl Street
New London, Conn.

A few samples of her entries might be of interest to our readers:

- December 25, 1940

The three boys, (Duncan, Joe and Ben) along with Mary Esther, and I took dinner with Jane and her family. After dinner Mary Esther took a few pictures. Late in the afternoon, Thurman, Jane, the three boys and Mary Esther went to Quakertown. Evelyn Cheesbro had a birthday cake for Joseph. They attended the Christmas tree entertainment at the school house. I spent the evening home. Melvia and Charles Watson spent the evening with me. We had prayer and I talked to him about the Lord.

- January 7, 1941

Duncan went back to school today (Zion Bible Institute). Edna Maxwell spent the afternoon and night with me. It was very cold today. I read the Bible and prayed but did not get the opportunity to wait on the Lord to the extent that I would have liked to. I talked from a portion of Psalm 105 and 106 at the young people's meeting.

- January 22, 1941

Mary Esther and I prayed. I had a real Spirit of prayer today. I went down Street this p.m. Bro & Sister Eddie Howard came. M.E. went to Jane's this p.m. – spent the night. Benjamin went with Bob skating – first time! I spent the evening alone. Wrote to Duncan & Joseph.

The entries only went to January 23, 1941 in this book.

Mary is in Waterford, Connecticut – Man is healed

A Christian Polish man was injured in a bad accident and taken to the hospital. Every bone in his foot was crushed. The hospital placed his foot in a cast and, as they could do nothing more for him, they sent him home.

After he arrived home, the pain became very severe and the family sent for Mary Crandall to come and pray for him. Mary asked her sister Jane and her husband Thurman to accompany her and they all went to the man's home and prayed for him. He was healed immediately. The family took his cast off and he began walking. He returned to the Doctors and showed them his foot. They took another x-ray and found that the bones in his foot were perfect, with no sign of ever being broken. This man testified to the healing power of the Lord!

Making maps for the bombing of Japan

(Excerpt from the publication 'After the night comes the morning' by Ben Crandall)

About this time brothers Joe and Benjamin felt it was their time to enroll in Bible school. But before they could leave and enroll, World War II had begun. Just as the war was starting Duncan went to Washington D. C. and got a job with the government. Then Ben followed him to Washington. People were coming from all over the United States to work in Washington because of the war. So at the young age of seventeen, Ben traveled along hoping to take classes in designing and drafting because this had been part of his background of studies during high school in New London.

When he checked into the classes he was told the government was in need of young men to take map-making classes, because our country was in trouble and lacked the skills necessary for the drawing of maps. Thankfully, they accepted Ben into the school for drafting and it wasn't long before his instructor at the school made him his assistant. Soon, he began helping the new students with enrolling and preparations for beginning drafting at this government school while he also continued his own classes there in drafting.

However it wasn't very long before the government school pulled Ben into a secret meeting and explained the absolute need for learning the map-making process. He also was told explicitly not to tell anyone where he would be working! There was a huge underground maze of rooms right below the classrooms in Washington D.C. where he was to work! Ben was completely amazed by this whole complex of tunnels and offices below.

Map making becomes drafting for the bombing of Japan:

It was also at this time that he began doing the drafting for the bombing of Japan. The job was to figure out the height of the mountains and hills of Japan and give them a few extra feet larger in case they get caught. There was a formula that was used for the drafting of this map. Every inch of Japan was configured in that room somewhere on paper and in the process of being mapped out! Every building and every road was shown and there was a translator who worked with them to put it all into English.

It was here that Ben worked, sometimes night and day, trying to complete the maps project he was given! Our map ended up being about 30 x 30 inches square which seemed to be really large to us at the time! It was actually describing an area 10 miles by 10 miles in Japan. At the center of every map was the target: target one, target two and target three. Three targets for them to bomb. Then all of a sudden there were changes in the war plans and now they were required to redo the whole map, to change this here and that over there.

It was during this period that Ben seemed to drift away from the Lord. He found a Pentecostal church in the Washington DC area and decided to visit it. But when he did visit, no one reached out and not even one person spoke to him!

Washington, D. C. Ben is in a difficult place

Duncan was working in another government office in Washington, but he worked different hours from Ben and wasn't nearby, and the hours were so strenuous and long that Ben had little time to see him. So he found himself without family or spiritual support during this period of his life and he began spending more and more time with his co-workers. During this time of living in Washington, D. C. Ben was drifting away and certainly not living for the Lord.

Ben found himself spending evenings with his work associates. They became friends and went out to the night clubs and began eating and drinking together on a regular basis. That was during a period of his life that Ben couldn't seem to stop and change what he was doing or how he was living. He did not contact his mother purposely because he did not wish her to know how he was living. However, God was speaking to his mother and she had a revelation that Ben was going to be drafted into the war effort. It all started when the Lord revealed to Mary how Ben was living. She said, "God, I cannot lose another son. I have already lost one son, I just cannot take it if I were to lose another son."

You see, Mary had been fasting and praying for three days. She never ate, she never went to bed, she just prayed nonstop for three days. My older sister Jane and others who were there told her to get up off the floor and to eat something. But she said, "I am not leaving this floor until I get the word that God has saved him." After three days she received the answer, she got up off the floor and went about her daily life in peace. And it was only days after that, when the Spirit moved on Ben one night, not in a church or anything like that, that he cried out to Jesus to forgive him of his sins and Ben became saved. It was a direct result of her prayers.

Ben recalls exactly where he was and what time it was:

"It was about three am in the morning, I was returning home on McArthur Blvd, in 1942. I began praying while walking home. I had been out all night with my friends and my girlfriend, when I began talking to God. I said, 'God, I can't change and I can't help myself either. There's no way I can live my life the right way for you in this tremendous city with its current of lifestyle.' So, I prayed that prayer asking forgiveness for my sins and I didn't feel a thing. But I did know that I had prayed earnestly and in faith! I went back home, got up the next day and my work associates began to call me once again to go out in the evenings with them. I simply replied that I 'didn't want' to go with them. I thought to myself if this lasts a week it is a miracle, because I had no desire to be out with them. After about two weeks they said to me, 'What happened to you? You are changed!' I replied, 'I am changed!' And I did not go out with them another time.

So I said to myself, 'If God can do this to me after just two weeks then I am going to go to Bible school. If God can do this for me then he can do this for anyone, so I am going to prepare myself by going to Bible school.'"

Mary was living in Waterford, Connecticut, at the time. One day, soon after Ben had had this life-changing experience, she was tending Jane's children while Jane went shopping for the family. That day, when Jane returned from shopping she found her mother stretched out on the floor. Jane quickly checked her pulse. Her body was warm so Jane knew that she was still alive.

Within a few minutes, Mary would rally and sit up fully conscious and awake. The Lord had taken Mary out of her body again and transported her to the office in Washington, D. C. where Ben and Duncan were working. Here she had heard that the whole group that was working there was to be shipped into the war zone. God had told Mary that the boys should come home immediately!

Mary conveyed this whole experience to Jane and asked her to wire the boys immediately to come home AT ONCE with no delay. They received the telegram that evening and the next morning they asked to be dismissed from their positions, and were granted the termination of their duties. The sudden change in Ben had not gone unnoticed, so when Ben went to tell his boss that he wanted to go to Bible school, he was not surprised. He said to me, 'Young man, there is a war going on right now and we are not letting anyone out! But you know what? I am going to release you! I am not supposed to release anyone, but I can still do that for you anyway...' So he did just that.

It was later that day that Ben learned that the afternoon of the same day the government drafted all his fellow employees into the Army, no exceptions! The officer in charge said "If you had waited until the end of today, I couldn't have let you go. We have just been commanded to freeze all positions at the end of the day. But, since you asked early, you may go."

Both young men returned to Connecticut, and it wasn't too long before they knew why God had given their mother this extraordinary experience. Every single man in that regiment was sent directly into the war zone and not one came back alive.

It was about this same time, in the fall of 1941, that Joseph enrolled at Zion Bible Institute in East Providence, Rhode Island. He graduated from there in 1943. When Joe was leaving his home, he got to the door and his mother called him back and said she had a 'word' for him. She raised her right hand and said, 'Behold!" I will show you what great things ye shall suffer for My name's sake." That was all. (Acts 9:16)

(And when Joe graduated from Zion, he started to walk off the platform... Sister Gibson called him back, raised her right had and said, "behold! I will show you what great things ye shall suffer for My name's sake.' That was all.)

So after being released from the work in Washington, Ben went home and applied to Zion Bible Institute late in that year, about November of 1943, and he was accepted into Bible School! World War II ended just about the time Ben graduated in 1945! Douglas had graduated in 1944. So three brothers went to Zion Bible Institute from 1941 to 1945. All three excelled, and were the speakers for graduation of their respective classes.

(this ends the excerpt from the publication 'After the night comes the morning' by Ben Crandall)

A Great Work is Begun in New York City by Benjamin Crandall

"This story really begins with my sister, Mary Esther, also an evangelist in the early days, and of how she became involved in the Brooklyn mission. One of the best things that ever happened to Mother in many years took place. Just as mighty vessels are guided through the pathless sea by small hidden rudders, so Mother's frail bark was guided by an unseen hand to a most likely port in the heart of Brooklyn, NY....

"It all began in the period right before the beginning of World War II, so it was about 1941. There was a preacher in New York whose wife was really impressed by Mary Esther Crandall. She really appreciated her, because she was a praying woman who had a wonderful testimony. So the preacher invited her to come to his meetings and speak, primarily to give her personal testimony. Then a lady named Sister Gomez, who saw her speak at that church, invited her to go to Brooklyn to also share her testimony at a very small storefront mission with a handful of people attending.

"Years ago, when my sister, Mary Esther, first saw the condition of the little mission in Brooklyn, she could see right away that they needed some help, and she knew my mother could help them by bringing some stability to their mission. My mother was the very definition of STEADY! She was as steady as the solid rock, and that is why she asked my mother to come. My mother really believed and knew in her heart that God had directly brought her there to the storefront mission in Brooklyn. When I came to see her at that Brooklyn mission, mother told me that God was going to do a great work there. Certainly the call of God to Brooklyn that was given to Mother Crandall in those early years was vindicated. . (This was part of a great work being done in the kingdom of God and it was a large part of Mother Crandall's destiny becoming fulfilled.)

"When Mary Esther visited this little mission house in Brooklyn, she began helping out there as she saw the needs of the people were great. Very quickly, she realized there was a problem going on with the director regarding some of the young girls at the mission. When Mary Esther saw that the director was fooling around with the girls at the Brooklyn Mission she said to herself, 'My mother needs to come here to this mission. They need to have someone like her to straighten this place out!' So Mary Esther called my mother in New London and asked her to come down to Brooklyn, New York, to help with the mission. Mary Esther continued working there herself. Soon, my mother arrived at the Brooklyn storefront mission and then moved her belongings into the back room of the mission as her living quarters. Word had gotten out about the bad behavior of the Brooklyn mission director regarding the young girls, so the director just pulled himself out before my mother even arrived and had a chance to meet him.

"The next problem to be dealt with was the Brooklyn mission overseers. They weren't sure they wanted a woman preacher ministering and directing at the mission. The leaders were strong. They were of one hundred percent Italian lineage, and were not used to having a woman preach. But my mother truly felt God had called her to come to this mission house in Brooklyn, and eventually the relationship worked out well between them." (In time they truly accepted this God fearing red-headed woman preacher who eventually became lovingly known by many as 'Mother Crandall'!)

Ben's visit to the mission in Brooklyn, NY

"I'll never forget how the old mission looked to me the first time I saw it. It was just before I graduated Bible School and Mother asked me to come down. I was now in my last year at Zion Bible Institute in 1945. As I stood there in the back of the storefront mission at 902 McDonald Avenue for the first time, my thought was, "Where in this world has Mother come to now?" I always knew Mother would do anything she thought she should do, and I knew she would go anywhere in this world if she thought the Lord wanted her to go. But surely - surely Mother isn't going to tell me the Lord sent her here!

"The old storefront mission was located at 902 McDonald Avenue under the 'El' (train tracks) next to the last store on the block and just before a large, unofficial garbage dump. It was during the war when city help was short. The lot beside the mission contained old mattresses, old beds, garbage, tin cans, broken-down baby carriages, general junk, plus hundreds of rats that seemed to shuttle back and forth between the lot and the mission storefront.

"As I got off the subway train and was heading to the mission I began to realize what a downtrodden area this storefront mission place was located in. The further I walked the worse it got. The closer I got to my mother's room in the back end of the mission, the more I was thinking about how terrible this place really was! There was a garbage dump right outside the building and so I imagined it smelled horribly too! By the looks of the mission, it was just a terrible looking, rundown, old dump of a place! There was dried paint running down the sides of the building, and you could see broken chairs from the outside.

"The inside of the mission wasn't much better. It was a tiny place, all of 19 feet wide. There were green curtains covering the glass front on each side of the door, and an old, dark, worn-out shade. You could stand on your tiptoes outside and see all that was going on inside. There were 48 broken-down old chairs, 24 on each side of the aisle. Adhesive tape and gobs of paint were holding up the enormous globe that hung over the minister's head, when someone stood to preach it looked something like 'Damocles' sword'.

"It was in a terrible mess everywhere so I thought to myself, "Where in the world has my mother ended up now? And then she came to the door and smiled at me like she was living on grand Fifth Avenue! She said to me, "GOD IS GOING TO DO A GREAT THING HERE!" And I thought to myself, "He will HAVE TO, from the looks of it! This place is a true dive!"

Eating on hotplates - McDonald Ave Mission House - Ben Crandall

"By this time Mother heard me and came out of the back room, her arms outstretched. She had been cooking for us on the hot plate with an apron tied around her, and was smiling from ear to ear. Happiness was written all over her face! It had been a long time since I had seen her that happy. She grabbed me and hugged and kissed me with a laugh of joy. Sometimes if I was a little shy about kissing her the way I should, she would say, "Aren't you going to kiss your 'old' Mother?"

"Mother couldn't have been happier if she had been showing me into the fanciest apartment on Park Avenue. She told me to stoop down so I wouldn't hit my head as we went into the back room, and then suggested I sit down while she finished cooking. The meal consisted of hamburgers, peas, whole wheat bread, a cup of light tea and a slice of A & P's plain cake. It was served out of old, broken, odd-and-end dishes that were kept in an orange crate nailed on the wall, but it was served with abundant love, kindness, faith and happiness, and was one of the greatest meals of my life. After we had eaten, Mother told me in glowing terms how God had led her to the mission at 902 (just as I had felt would be the case) to continue her gospel work to those who wanted to hear it.

"Mother definitely felt called of the Lord to return to Brooklyn and to stay there for her remaining life's work. So she moved into the little mission there under the "El" (elevated train tracks) at 902 McDonald Avenue. This was where Mother Crandall prayed, worked and lived out her later years of life!"

Guys are drunk at the Mission on McDonald Avenue.

Some of the neighborhood guys who were not exactly committed to the Lord would get drunk in the bars until they were plastered. But, then they were unable to go home drunk and plastered to their families. So they would come up to Mother Crandall's apartment and pray with Mary until they sobered up and were able to go home. They were from families that attended the church but usually did not attend themselves. They were appreciative and respectful of Mother Crandall and her help. She would always take time to help them. It was about this time that people began to call Mary Crandall, "Mother Crandall," and looked to her as a supportive caring, praying woman of God who could be counted upon to encourage them like a mother.

Ben's graduation and move to Brooklyn with his wife, Jeanne:

"A few months had passed since I visited Brooklyn. In the spring of 1945, I was graduating from Zion Bible Institute and of course, my mother came to see me graduate! Then she went back down to Brooklyn and called me. She said, "You know, I think God could use you and Jeanne in this mission! I think you should come here to Brooklyn." My wife Jeanne and I had just gotten married in July, in Littleton, Maine. However, we both said to her, "We'll go." We visited with my sister Jane for a few days in and then joined Mother very soon afterwards at the mission. It was still 1945."

Ben and Jeanne went to Brooklyn to rent a place of their own but money quickly ran out. It wasn't long before they had moved onto the floor of the mission and Mary was living in the back room of the mission. They had a mattress behind the curtains and pulled it out at night for the couple to sleep upon. There was one hot plate that they cooked all their food on for the three of them and they took turns cooking. About $20.00 came in as an offering to live off of during the week which meant they only had a couple of dollars for food each day, so they ate basically the same thing every day.

That small mission was the early beginnings of what would become a great work for the Kingdom of God, and it is still a great work that is going on until this very day! Today between 2000 and 3000 people attend the church that came out of that little mission. And many churches sprang forth from that church. It is a sending church, sending missionaries and leaders out to start new works all the time.

Revival came to that little mission that first year. It was not long before they had outgrown that little building at 902 McDonald Avenue. Within the mission were a couple of men who gave large tithes of money and one of them believed if he left the mission that the work would fold up. He left because of some disagreement with the leadership. However, the mission did not fold up. In fact it began to grow and some wonderful folk began to come and join the mission, including Sister Minor who was a lovely Christian lady from the Alliance (Missionary) Church who had received the Baptism of the Holy Ghost. After her, many others followed and began to join up with the mission house. Within a year the gathering had grown to about 100 new people attending the mission. Now it became so crowded that the latecomers could not even get into the building in Brooklyn at 902 McDonald Ave, between 18th Ave. and Ave. F. because it was packed with new people.

Joseph's children have a terrible accident

Joe Crandall had graduated from Zion in 1943 and married Marge Watrous. A terrible accident occured involving their three young children in 1949. Joe and Marge Crandall lived in an old farm house in Ledyard, Connecticut in an area called Quakertown. Jane was visiting with Joe and Marge at that time. They had not lived there long when a potentially tragic event happened. The prior resident had been a veterinarian and had accidentally left a supply of medicine in the attic. Unbeknownst to the parents, three of their children, Rosemary, Margaret and little Joe Jr. crawled up into the attic and got into a substance called bi-chloride of mercury. This acid will eat through iron.

The children returned downstairs and fell into an unnatural sleep. Marge noticed this and spoke to Jane about it. Jane noticed that something was terribly wrong. At midnight Marge saw Joe Jr.'s eye was in bad shape. Little Joe's eye condition deteriorated and they rushed him to the hospital. His whole eye turned white and came out on his cheek bone. His lips were swollen out of proportion. He was screaming and went into convulsions. They had to strap him down. His mother, Marge, couldn't handle all the trauma and fainted.

The doctor told them that his eye was gone and that he might lose the other one. He said that his throat and esophagus were in very bad condition and that he may not last throughout the night. In fact, all three children were in very serious condition.

Joe and Marge went to Jane and Thurman's home to pray. Mary was living in Brooklyn but had come to Connecticut to visit, and by now was praying with them also, along with Johnny Harvey. At some point there were a total of six people who were praying and could not eat, sleep or cook until they heard something from heaven. Marilyn Maxwell, who was a little tot, was as quiet as can be during this time of prayer. It was like a holy hush had come over the household.

The group was praying in the living room, and at 4 a.m. Mother Crandall finally spoke and said, "Well, we can stop praying now and start praising God, for He has heard!"

At first, their father Joe couldn't accept it. His children were in grave danger. But, shortly God gave him the assurance that everything was going to be all right. He left at 5 am for the hospital. The doctors and nurses were there, standing around the desk. "Joe, "they said, "We are so glad you are here because we don't know what to write on this chart. Your child is healed! He's in perfect shape – come and look!" Baby Joe's eyes were perfect. He was perfectly whole, sitting up in his crib, playing with a toy car. Rosemary and Margaret were healed at the same time. They were all healed and went home that afternoon.

Following this healing, their doctor who was a Jewish man, called Joe into his office and said, "Rev. Crandall, I would like for you to tell me about your God, about your belief in Him. A miracle has happened, and it was nothing we did". Joe had the opportunity to tell him about the power of prayer in the Christian's life.

An A & P grocery store becomes the new church, Calvary Tabernacle

Back to Brooklyn: In 1950 the church asked Rev. Benjamin Crandall to become pastor and he prayerfully accepted the challenge to lead this growing, young, dynamic congregation! However, Mary Crandall would continue to be a vital part of this church throughout the years to come. In the years that followed, Ben and Jeanne Crandall along with Mother Crandall, worked and labored together at Calvary Tabernacle. Certainly the call of God to Brooklyn that was given to Mary Crandall in those early years was vindicated. Ben Crandall was the pastor for 40 years taking over where Mother Crandall left off.

Several of Mary Crandall's friends were prayer warriors, who would get together for a time of prayer frequently. Mary ran the Morning Prayer meetings for years along with Sister Mini Intaglia. Mini saw that Jeanne and Ben were sleeping on the floor. So she gave the $1,000 she had saved up with her husband by running a little dry cleaning business to help them buy a house. (That would be close to $20k or $30k today!) She gave this to Ben's family to find a place to live. However, ultimately they used it for a down payment on the (A & P grocery store at 946-948 McDonald Avenue) for a new church facility because they needed more room. It was perfect timing for helping with the down payment on what was then an A & P grocery store. The overgrown storefront mission needed a new home and this building looked like just the right place!

It was a nice three story building. They had the money for the mortgage but needed to put several thousand dollars down in order to close the title. And they still needed an additional $3,000 or $4,000 more to move into the building. When the day came for the closing costs of the building the church did not have one penny for the closing.

At that time there was a man who was attending the mission who was from Italy, a first generation Italian. He spoke very little English, and did not seem well off at all. He came to Ben after hearing of the financial need and said, "Brother Crandall, come and take me to the bank." So they went to the bank and he withdrew his life savings, or most of it, in order to help out and allow the little church to move. They got to the bank just in time with the money before their closing time. Because of the significant help this man was in the hour of need, they wanted to be able to give back to him in some way. So they prepared a room for him upstairs in the mission house that was going to be completely his own. Immediately after that on his own accord, he began sweeping the floors of the church and keeping the chairs in good order. These were things that he had never been asked to do for the new church, but they were very grateful to him for it.

The little congregation made some repairs on the A & P Grocery store, put new windows in it and got the new church building in much better condition than when it was first purchased. They raised the money from their church members who in turn also made the repairs on the building. The church was able to stay at that location for quite a few years. There were four apartments upstairs. Mary Crandall lived in one and the Italian man lived in the other. They were able to rent out the other two apartments which helped out financially. God was able to do many great works in this A & P building that had become the new home, and the little church had a new name: "Calvary Tabernacle!"

Calvary Tabernacle Church moves again

Several years had passed and there was a period when Ben was praying and fasting concerning his mother-in-law who had cancer. During this time God began to speak to Ben concerning the over packed church. They had once again outgrown their church building that was meeting at the A & P grocery store on 946-48 McDonald Avenue and were in need of a new building.

As Ben tells the story, he believed that God said to him, "I am going to give you the land you need for your building." In order for this to happen Ben was going to need some help. There was a wealthy man in the church who was a building contractor with great experience. He also owned trucks, land, and an excellent corner lot. Ben believed God showed him that this was the man who was going to help the church, but how could Ben approach him to tell him that? Then one day he came to Ben and said, "You know, I believe God is saying to me that I am to give you my corner lot. I had been planning to retire with this lot, but now I sense God is saying for me to give you this land for your church!"

When the time came to build the new church this same man served as the general contractor. He hired the laborers and he kept an itemized list of the contracting materials he spent on it. When the time came for the mortgage to be paid, they were able to pay off the debt that was owed him from their current mortgage. The address to this building was 7th Avenue and 64th Street in Bay Ridge, New York. This new building was able to hold over 700 people although there were only 200 church members at that time. They wondered "Will we ever fill this church building up?" In 1963 the beautiful new building at 7th Avenue and 64th Street was completed and the growing congregation was able to move into it.

Mother Crandall's witnessing

Because of Mary Duncan's experience she never quit praying and she never quit witnessing. There have been very few like her! She would go into the subway and she never sit down, because she gave a tract to everybody on the car. Some would throw them on the floor, some would take it, some would sneer at it, but that never stopped her for a minute. When others stepped onto a train with her, they had to have courage, because one never knew what was going to happen! Of course, immediately out would come her salvation tracts and there she was witnessing again... Anyone who came to the house, she would encourage them with a word of scripture and would witness to them about Jesus. She would never change from this platform. Later in life, even when she went shopping with her grandchildren, she would give out a tract to the saleslady and witness to those around her about her Lord.

For example, witnessing even took place right in the middle of a funeral service. When she was in a service she would stand up and tell the "attendees" about Jesus, and how they could receive heaven and not the hell in their afterlife. She was a walking, talking "living testimony" for her savior. And nothing could stop her from telling everyone about it. She had a passion for the lost like no one you have ever seen. This passion was her life, all of her life! There was nothing she would NOT do to help keep people out of an eternity of torture in hell.

Literally thousands were won to Christ because of Mary's witnessing. Years after Mary had left this earth, one of Mary's nephews asked an outstanding Methodist minister who had greatly impressed him, "How were you converted?" His answer was, "Have you ever heard of a young, redheaded woman evangelist by the name of Mary Duncan? I was converted while attending one of her revival meetings when I was a young man."

Mother Crandall

This section of the book contains stories and recollections of Mary Duncan Crandall by family members during this period of her life...

Recollection from Douglas Crandall about his Grandmother Crandall:

My earliest recollection of Grandma Crandall is going to her apartment on McDonald Ave. in Brooklyn, which was beside our church. She lived in the back apartment, on the first floor, up above the Italian Restaurant. To reach it, you had to go up a long flight of stairs since the first floor had very tall ceilings. We lived two streets over in Brooklyn on East 3rd Street between Avenue F and Ditmus Avenue. The elevated railway train passed above the apartment house Grandma lived in. I remember the musty smell of her apartment, including the Kitchen, living room, bedroom and bathroom. There was a closet in the hallway leading into the apartment and it was always packed with old clothes, from the 1940s and the 1950s. Grandma stayed up late; never got to bed until 1:00 or 2:00 in the morning; and never got up and around until 1:00 or so in the afternoon.

She wore big black, clunky shoes and thick support stockings; typical boot type shoes from the 1930s… She would have a boiled egg at noon and shredded wheat, a piece of toast and Postum or tea. (Postum is a powdered roasted-grain beverage once popular as a coffee substitute, made popular during the war.) She always had her glass of milk in the afternoon.

Recollection from Marlene Watrous Cunningham:

As a young girl, I enjoyed taking the train to NYC and staying with Grandmother Crandall in her Brooklyn apartment; hearing the train go by overhead and eating orange ice-cream pop ups from the deli. She also helped me memorize my first scripture while riding in a car with my family when I was about 6 or 7 years old. It was, John 14:6. Jesus answered, "I am the way the truth and the life. No one comes to the Father except through me." She also corrected my grammar one time comparing the difference between 'bring' and 'take' when I was about nine years old. She made me use examples over and over until she thought I had it down pat.

Grandma's Prayer pillows from Doug Crandall:

People went up to the apartment for prayer and she would get out of bed and pray with them, and go back to bed if it was still morning. Her life was praying all the time. Whenever anybody came to see her she had to have a word of prayer with them before they left … "a word of prayer' was an ominous phrase… because the prayers could take quite a long time and cover many bases.. She had two couches that faced one another. They were the high old -fashioned stuffed sofas, and each had pillows underneath them. These were her prayer pillows. When it came time to pray, out came the pillows and they all kneeled down on them. Any time I saw the pillows come out I was gone… I would run as fast as I could.

Harry's single sister, Daisy, lived close to Mary Crandall's' home in New London

Mary's Daughter, Mary Esther often went to help their Aunt Daisy Crandall, sister to Harry Crandall, when Aunt Daisy was in her later years. She had a small, lovely home in New London, Connecticut, not far from Mary Crandall's house on Vauxhall Street. Mary Esther and her daughter Marlene, in her teens, would grocery shop and do small errands for her whenever possible. She had the most beautiful flower garden ever according to Marlene.

Doug Crandall Grocery shopping for Grandma Crandall:

"I would go shopping for grandma once a week, usually after school on Friday. When I was 11 years old (she was 75 yrs old.) I would go home and mother would send me to the church office where my dad would give me a list of items and some cash (maybe $10) to go shopping for Grandma. I went down the stairs, up the stairs, down the stairs and back up again to get it done! The list did not vary... one frying chicken, one pound of hamburger, onion, carrots, celery, rice, once in a while a piece of steak, or a pork chop or two, half a dozen eggs, two packages of frozen peas and carrots, rarely frozen corn, a small loaf of Pepperidge Farm's dark whole wheat bread, shredded wheat cereal, red jello, chocolate ice cream, one stick of butter, one quart of whole milk, one quart of butter milk, and a quart of chocolate milk. I went to the butcher first, then to the deli for the other items. At the deli you gave them the list and they assembled the items on the list for you.

While I was shopping for her, she would get all her dirty clothes into the laundry bag. Down the stairs and across 18th Avenue was a Chinese laundry. She told me to take it to the wet wash (as opposed to the dry cleaning). They would wash it, dry and fold it, and place it back into the bag. I would pick it up on Saturday and deliver it back to Grandma that day."

When grandma was ready to cook her food she would stew the chicken in the pot with her rice and vegetables. Then she was able to eat from it throughout the week. If she had company she would have food brought home from the Chinese restaurant or Italian restaurant to share with her company. She liked a little Chinese food from time to time from the Free World Restaurant down the block. They always brought her back some egg fu-yang, wonton soup, and a little fried rice, too. That would last her for two or three meals. Or if she wanted Italian food it was always just spaghetti and meatballs. There was no variety there, either. She never ate in the restaurants. She always had me or someone else take it home to her. She lived in a very simple world when she was older.

Remembrance from Arlene Crandall Jacobs

When Grandma Crandall would come to visit us she always would share how the Lord would speak to her about what to do next in life. She wanted to know the will of the Lord ahead of time. Then she would pray as if she knew that it would be exactly as God planned it for her. She would always be praising our Lord Jesus with rolling her R's with Prrraise the Lord or Prrraise you Jesus. I did learn this from her: to be always "thankful" and "Praise" the Lord at all times no matter what!

Mother Crandall's way of relating to others:

The neighborhood was largely Italians in ethnicity. They were second generation Italians, and Mother Crandall had great difficulty pronouncing Italian names. She butchered their names. She had a hard time with Italian names. She would 'anglicize' everything. And she always kept her southern accent. If names ended in a vowel, it gave her trouble. Italian names really challenged her. Salvatore was just Saul (Sol). But they all loved her anyway.

She had her glass of milk in the afternoon. There was no coffee for her in the daytime. She was greatly loved by the people. She preached for several years in most of the services when she started the new church in Brooklyn. But Ben increasingly spoke the messages until in 1950 the church appointed him their pastor. Mary continued to preach from time to time, but her main focus became the prayer ministry and special prayer meetings among the people of the church.

Mother Crandall

Mother Crandall's later years according to Ben Crandall

As she aged, her travels became more and more localized, finally becoming limited to within a two blocks area most of the time, except for trips to Connecticut and one trip each winter to North Carolina to stay with her daughter, Jane, in Falcon, North Carolina. She would stay in the south for a couple of months each winter. Soon after Christmas, no later than early January, she would get on the train and head south to Falcon, returning about the end of March. When the daffodils broke ground in the Carolinas she knew it was time to head back north to New York.

After returning to the north, she stayed with Ben's family on Narrows Avenue a few days and then she went back to Connecticut for the rest of the summer. She was living with her children here and there because all the apartments that had belonged to Ben's church in NYC had been eliminated. Ben would later buy his mother a house on Vauxhall Street in New London, Connecticut so she would have a place to call home. It would be her residence until she passed on from this life.

Jane's story of her Mary going to Hong Kong

When Jane left for a missionary term in Hong Kong in 1963, she asked herself, "Will I ever see my mother again?" It was to be a seven-year long mission term. "Yes, I would," Jane would later learn...

The reader will recall that Mary had felt a real call to go to China as a missionary when she was a young lady. It was a burden for the people of China that she carried all her life. Little did she suspect that she would be able to realize that dream late in her life. Mother Crandall was now living in New London, Connecticut, in her little home on Vauxhall Street at that time. Mary Esther often visited along with others. So it was in 1968, at the age of 80, Mother Crandall consented to go to Hong Kong, even though she told Jane that she wasn't sure she should go. Ben knew that deep down Mary had always wanted to go to China as a missionary, since she had been a young woman, so his church helped pay for her trip.

When Mary arrived and saw such beautiful, huge mountains, she was overwhelmed with God's handiwork. "Oh, how I want Ben to see this," she remarked often throughout her time there. While in Hong Kong, Jane and Thurman took Mary up on a lookout mountain that overlooked communist China. This was a spot where tour busses always stopped. This particular day there was a Jewish doctor, who practiced medicine in NY, visiting this location in Hong Kong. Of course Mary told him the story of salvation, and he accepted the Lord as his savior. Time passed. The tour group returned to NY.

Mary later heard that this doctor called all of his staff into his office to tell them of his experience in Hong Kong. It so happened that one of the doctors on his staff happened to be Mary's nephew by marriage, so they found out in this way about the "Rest of the Story".

But in 1969 Mary's health was continuing to decline and her sugar problem was bothering her much more. After a while she felt her health was getting to be a problem and that perhaps she should return to the US and closer to the family. But how could she get home? Some insight into her situation may be gained from including this excerpt from a letter written to her by her daughter Mary Esther at that time:

"...I've had something flash before me, much like the recalling of a dream which I believe the Lord has revealed concerning the way He is going to open for you to come home.

It was that folks (I would say, maybe friends of the family) made a trip over to Hong Kong and that rather unexpectedly, you have come back over here (to the US) with them. And it all seemed to be the plan of the Lord for your coming back with them. You seemed to have made the trip really well, and you were really happy and looking good!

So, Mom, I'm sure God has His way and His time for getting you back. But right now, possibly, He still has a place of service for you over there. However, stay prepared, for when He should make the way for you to come back, you'll be ready."

When it was time for her to return home to the US, Leroy Frazier, Edna (Maxwell's) husband, brought her home from China. When she returned to the US, Mary's son Joseph went to New York to pick her up and take her to his home in Sarasota, Florida. Much later, Mother Crandall was very sick and Jane and Thurman brought her to their home in Falcon, North Carolina. Ben oversaw her being placed into a nursing home, while Jane and Thurman got settled back into their own home in Falcon, NC.

Mary's health deteriorates by Jane Maxwell

One evening in North Carolina Mary and the others were having a prayer meeting in a doctor's home and the doctor got saved. But Mary had an acute gall bladder attack, and she had many gall stones. After examining Mary, the doctor said the gall bladder had erupted many years before and her body created a calcium bag to form around them to protect itself. He said he had never seen anything like that before. She also had a sugar problem and the doctor sat up with her the whole night. "God brought her through," Jane recalls later on.

But as the months progressed Mother Crandall's health kept deteriorating and she would exclaim, "I just can't make it like this. I want to go to my heavenly home!" Three days before she died, Mary said, "Jane, the Lord showed me I was going home in three days." In three days she had a setback and was taken to the hospital in Sanford, North Carolina.

Mother Crandall had the Crandall body type...toothpick legs and heavy on top. She was very inactive in her last years, and had become large. She had an enlarged heart and did not like to go downstairs to leave her place. Friends tried to make her get out, but she resisted. She became sick her last year of life and ended up a little while in a nursing home in Falcon, North Carolina. She remained with her daughter Jane, and her husband Thurman in Sanford, North Carolina where she passed away into the arms of her Savior. The family was all there. She was conscious to the very end. A lady came in to pray for her minutes before she died and Mary spoke in tongues and gave the lady a prophecy. Mary looked up into heaven and gave a big smile. She just peacefully went to sleep in Jesus! She died on January 16, 1971 in Sanford, NC.

Mother Crandall Goes Home - Ben Crandall's recollections

"The kitchen phone rang at 6:10 Saturday evening. Karen, my daughter, answered and in a frightened voice said, 'Dad, it's for you - it's long distance.' For days now, I had approached each phone call with apprehension and reluctance, bracing myself for the news. I walked slowly to the phone, thinking, 'This is probably it!' The operator asked, 'Is this Rev. Crandall?' I answered, 'Yes, this is he.' The next voice I heard was my brother Joe. In a deep, sober voice he said, 'Mother is failing fast and has been asking for all her children and wants to see you.'

"I decided I would leave by plane immediately, and hurried off to buy a few things I needed for the trip. Meanwhile, my wife Jeanne called Grace, my secretary, to start making arrangements for my absence on Sunday. I rounded corners faster than usual coming home; I 'gave it the gas' down our Narrows Avenue in Brooklyn where we lived, and swung to the curb in front of the house. When I got out of the car, I noticed Jeanne looking out of the tiny front window – something she never does. I thought, 'Why isn't she packing my suitcase or calling someone on the phone, or doing something?' I opened the front door ... Jeanne had a strange look on her face and the atmosphere was quiet. As I started to speak, Jeanne said, 'She's gone.' I repeated her words half under my breath, 'She's gone?' 'Yes,' answered Jeanne, 'You had barely driven off when the phone rang again ... it was Max and he said Mother had died. You are to call him back as soon as you can.' I turned slowly to the same small window and looked out.

"Now I understood why I felt as I did that Wednesday after Christmas - I had gone to see Mother on Monday, and on Wednesday, when I came to say good-bye, there was a strange sinking feeling in me that that was the last time I would ever see Mother in this world. Jane, the sister with whom Mother was staying, and I had previously decided I should just go quietly and not make too much of saying good-bye. We were afraid my leaving would upset her. I walked into her room, and as I kissed her and stroked her forehead and reddish-golden hair, under my breath I said, 'Good-bye Mother, I'll see you in heaven.' Then I turned and walked straight to the door. She called, 'Ben, you aren't going, are you?' But I couldn't answer - I wanted to go back in there and hold my tired, weary mother close in my arms, but I just couldn't. She was too sick for that. Instead, with my jaw set, I forced myself to walk out the back door to the car.

"To myself I said, 'You will have to act like a man even though you don't feel very much like one.' I was full of mixed emotions as I tore myself away from the small window. I returned Max's phone call and began piecing together the details. I was not completely satisfied until many hours later when I visited the hospital for myself and stood reverently in Mother's room, 203.

"At 6:55 that previous Saturday evening, back in North Carolina the day was just ending - it was getting dark outside. The last tinge of rosy light was fading swiftly from the west as the stars began one after another to burst through the dark blue velvet sky. The wind whispered softly through the tall pines outside, letting us know the day was over and night had come. Upstairs, Joe stepped quietly into the room. Sister Comfort, a close friend of Mother's, was by the window; Joe was between Mother and the door. The others had gone out. Mother recognized Joe and said, 'Joe, come closer so I can see you, come up closer Joe.' Joe went to her side and began gently to stroke her brow. Mother had been so weak she could hardly lift her head, and her voice was just a whisper. Then suddenly she lifted up her head; her eyes opened wide and became alert - not staring, but seeing. Joe said later, 'I could never adequately describe that moment, but I knew she saw past the little room - far beyond all the surroundings of earth - far into eternity. She gazed with great amazement and then calmly laid her head down, closed her eyes and fell asleep.' Mother's long day and the day outside had closed together.

"New plans had to be made - the plane reservation was cancelled and a call placed for Douglas, my son, and another for Duncan, my brother whom we had not yet reached. Douglas would catch the first plane out of Providence or Boston and as soon as he arrived we would all leave for Cromartie Funeral Home in Dunn, North Carolina, where we all had agreed to meet. The funeral was held on Monday afternoon at 2:30 in the Culbreth Memorial Church, Falcon, North Carolina."

Life Lesson from Mary Duncan Crandall - FORGIVENESS
(This is an excerpt from one of Mary's sermons, titled "The Extent of Forgiveness")

"God has not left us in ignorance as to the extent of forgiveness (with) which we are to extend toward our fellowmen. Christ's (forgiveness) was 'seventy times seven,' and Paul said, 'even as God for Christ's sake hath forgiven you.' (This) shows that our forgiveness must be full and hearty. There is no room – whatever the injury – for a Christian to have a grudge nestling in his heart against any human being. As God meets the forgiven sinner, 'remembering his transgressions against him no more forever,' so much at our forgiveness place the forgiven again in our hearts and (be) fully restored to our affections and care. Many will say, 'Yes, I forgive him; but … There is no 'but' in forgiveness. 'Well, I have nothing against him, but I don't want to have anything to do with him,' is a contradiction. Christian forgiveness is not a legal thing, but a matter of the heart's outgoing (life) to be right with every living being. Brother, to be forgiven is to forgive. I hope you are forgiven."

Forgiveness by Benjamin Crandall

"The full value of a life often cannot be found in the material things left behind that we can see, but is found instead in the spiritual that eludes the casual eye. Among my most prized possessions is a picture of Mother I have hanging in the hidden chambers of my heart; a picture of 'Forgiveness'. As a boy, this picture was very distasteful. Later, I came to realize its infinite value. The picture is Mother teaching us to love and respect our father - the man who had deserted her and left her alone with six small children. A father we did not know and whom I had never seen until I was a teenager. Mother was successful, for when I met my father for the first time, at age 14, I loved him! As an adult understanding the circumstances, I realized this was a masterpiece of Christian love and 'forgiveness.' I cherish this picture today and realize the reward my Mother will have in the kingdom of God."

Mary's Legacy

Even though Mary Duncan Crandall has passed on to her eternal reward, her ministry will continue until the end of time through a host of people whose lives she touched and blessed. What could become of this little red-haired baby, the twelfth child of a cotton-farming preacher, born after the Civil War into poverty and with no education? Whatever could she hope to accomplish with her life? Would her life make any difference at all?

Well, sir, Mary Duncan Crandall directly touched the lives of thousands of people, and through her lineage and spiritual motherhood literally is still touching lives of tens of thousands even today. Several churches were established. Evangelists called into their ministries. Missionaries called into the field around the world. Thousands were born again.

She had heard clearly from God those words so long ago; truly she was obedient to God's orders to "Go, warn them to flee from the wrath to come. Go! Go!" As a result, tens of thousands of people have escaped from the fire of hell and are destined to spend eternity in paradise with their Lord and Savior, Jesus Christ. No doubt there was a long line of happy people waiting there to thank her in person. I know all of us in her family will be there to thank her face to face someday!

Mary Duncan Crandall 1888 – 1971

Acknowledgments

This brief sketch of the life of Mary Duncan Crandall could not have been assembled without the help of many of her family. There were so many stories from her life that some had to be left out. I hope I have selected those that best inform us who she was and how she lived by faith when that was all she had.

- Special thanks goes to Rev. Benjamin Crandall for a lot of narration and many stories from his own memory. When this was written he was the last of her living children.
- To Joseph Crandall for leaving us written and spoken stories about his remarkable mother and her impact on his ministry.
- To Jane Crandall Maxwell for many childhood stories and memories.
- To Patricia Pickard for transcribing Jane Crandall Maxwell's stories along with biographical and genealogical information back in 1995 in hopes of a book to be written about Mother Crandall. Perhaps this is that book.
- To Harold and Marge Maxwell for loaning me all of Patricia Pickard's materials.
- Mary Edith Watrous Sheckler for loaning me so many old photographs from Mother Crandall's life.
- Debbie Watrous Sherwood for loaning me so many old family photos.
- Thanks also goes to all the grandchildren for sharing your personal memories of Grandma Mary Duncan Crandall.
- Maria Woodworth-Etter, *Signs and Wonders,* Whitaker House, 1997.
- Michael Thornton, *Fire in The Carolinas, The Revival Legacy of G. B. Cashwell and A. B. Crumpler*, Creation House, 2014.
- Rev. Benjamin Crandall, *It Took a Miracle*, Zions Bible Institute, 1996.
- Joe McIntyre, *E.W. Kenyon, and His Message of Faith, The True Story,* Charisma House, 1997.
- Thank you Phil Cunningham for all your historical research, writing and so very much time and editing.

--- Marlene Watrous Cunningham

About the author

Marlene Watrous Cunningham was born and reared in the beautiful coastal area of eastern Connecticut around Ledyard and Mystic, Connecticut. Her mother was Mary Esther Crandall Watrous (third child of Mary Duncan Crandall) and her father was Cornelius Benjamin Watrous. She graduated from a Christian private boarding high school in Zellwood Florida, named Hampden Du Bose Academy in 1974.

She attended both Bob Jones University and Oral Roberts University and graduated from ORU in Tulsa, Oklahoma in 1976. She holds a degree in Elementary Education, with Art and French minors. She taught in elementary and middle school for about 10 years in both public and private schools in the Tulsa area.

In 1974 she married Gary Tedder, a member of the World Action Singers from Oral Roberts University and they had one son, Ryan, in 1979. They were divorced after nine years of marriage. Marlene married Phil Cunningham in 1986, who has two daughters, Tamra and Michele. As of the time of this book Marlene and Phil have been married 31 years, and they now have 6 children (counting spouses), 8 grandchildren (counting spouses) and one great grandson.

She resides in Tulsa with her husband where she is Executive Director of Harvest House Outreach Inc., a nonprofit that provides groceries, clothing, transportation assistance, infant services, utility bill payment help and prescription eyeglasses to the less fortunate. It is funded by private donations and many wonderful foundations. In her free time Marlene loves to travel, oil paint, lunch with friends and visit her children and grandchildren! Oh, and to ride in a classic convertible car with her husband Phil on a beautiful Oklahoma day!!

She is grateful to have been given the opportunity to write this book so you too can know this wonderful woman named Mary Duncan Crandall, who was her maternal grandmother. She hopes you will be encouraged by the book.

If you want to drop her a line you may do so by email at: mar.007@att.net . Marlene sends God's richest blessings to each one of you!!!

Marlene Watrous Cunningham

Made in the USA
San Bernardino, CA
09 December 2017